*Advance Praise for*
## TAROT DECODED

"Elizabeth Hazel's *Tarot Decoded* brings astrological dignity to the modern tarot. A concise and intelligent framework for both amplifying and contextualizing readings via modal, elemental, numeric, zodiacal and planetary affinities, this book presents the fine tunings and occult panache necessary to transpose home-spun, three chord Tarot songs into full symphonic depth and resonance. The result is music to the divinatory imagination."

—ART ROSENGARTEN, PH.D.,
author of *Tarot and Psychology*

"*Tarot Decoded* presents original and welcome methods of synthesizing tarot and astrology. It is a book for which the time has definitely come. With techniques and exercises, some based on metaphysical writings a century old, and others that are all her own, Elizabeth Hazel integrates the two pursuits in innovative and exciting ways.

If you, like myself, are a person passionate about both tarot and astrology, you have probably read numerous top-notch astrology books as well as many excellent books on the tarot, but have found a dearth of material combining the two subjects. This book is the first to step unabashed into that void and to provide many thought-provoking avenues for a successful and rewarding integration of the two arcane sciences.

For those proficient with tarot, but versed in only rudimentary astrology, Hazel's material will walk you carefully through enough basic material to have you up and running. I predict that this book will make tarotists who have previously only dabbled in astrology want to learn more, in order to continue to combine the systems for increased depth and detail in their readings."

—VALERIE SIM-BEHI,
Vice President of Communications for
the American Tarot Association,
editor of *Tarot Reflections* and *The ATA Quarterly*,
and author of
*The Comparative Tarot Deck* and *Tarot Outside the Box*

"Reading *Tarot Decoded* is like attending a series of graduate seminars with the dean of the Tarot Astrology Academy. In fact, the book would make a fine text for a study group. Liz's sense of humor puts some of the more haughty court cards in their place, and her descriptions of the four elements are sheer poetry. She reminds us that the tarot world of dignities is filled with friendly and hostile neighbors who fine-tune a card's intentions. Her unique spreads and explanations of dignities will certainly provide you with new ways to understand yourself and your clients. Liz Hazel brings us to a new level of understanding the world of tarot astrology."

—SANDRA A. THOMSON, CTGM,
President of the American Tarot Association

"In reading *Tarot Decoded* by Elizabeth Hazel I was both impressed and challenged—impressed by the depth and scope of what Hazel presents in her ground-breaking book, and challenged to expand my mind to a new and exciting way of interpreting the tarot.

Being an avid astrologer, as well as a tarot professional, I happily found Elizabeth's book to be a blend of both disciplines, all of which was written in a cohesive and holistic manner. Her many years of study are evident by the wealth of information included and the numerous examples given.

*Tarot Decoded* unlocks new material to aid the tarot practitioner as well as the tarot scholar. This book belongs on every serious tarot student's shelf.

Bravo, Liz!"

—JANET BERRES,
author of *Textbook of the Tarot*

"Elizabeth Hazel's *Tarot Decoded* is a very special contribution to the literature in this field. The work is both original and knowledgeable, reflecting many years of experience and thought. Her dual expertise in astrology and the tarot shines through with simple and readable explanations of how the two strands of spiritual study can be blended in doing readings with the cards. It is a fine crossover text for tarot students who want to know more astrology and for astrology lovers who want to know more tarot."

—DONNA CUNNINGHAM, internationally-known
astrologer and metaphysical author of
*How to Read Your Astrological Chart,*
*The Moon in Your Life,* and
*The Consulting Astrologer's Guidebook*

"Elizabeth Hazel has created a delightful book that applies the ancient wisdom of astrology to learning tarot divination. Her book provides a useful analysis of the cards in relation to sun signs, planets, and elements, making it easy for an astrologer to learn tarot or a tarot reader to learn astrology. Also, it offers the most thorough treatment of the relationships of cards in a spread to each other now available, with demonstration readings to show how to put her lessons into practice. Whether you want to learn how to give tarot readings or improve your tarot skills, this book is a great companion to open a new door to deeper understanding."

—KOOCH & VICTOR DANIELS,
authors of *Tarot d'Amour*

"Elizabeth Hazel's *Tarot Decoded* is an amazing accomplishment. Hazel has taken the accumulation of years of study and expertise and synthesized them into an articulate and well-developed book on tarot. Even people who have studied tarot, astrology, and alchemy for many years will find much new in this book.

Although the knowledge presented in this book is impressive, what is even more outstanding is the variety and flexibility of uses for dignities in the book: elemental dignities, modal dignities, numeric dignities and more, all presented with practical examples and versatile spreads. The beginning student of tarot will find the chapter on the elements an incredible primer that will provide an excellent groundwork for future study. The intermediate and advanced students of tarot will find the chapters on using the tarot with astrology and numerology to be sound and workable. Hazel has a brilliant mind and a wealth of knowledge, but her work is always grounded in practicality.

This is a book to read and study, a book to reflect on, a book to re-read and to keep as a reference. I highly recommend it for any serious student of the tarot. I plan to use it as a required text for my intermediate and advanced tarot students."

—NINA LEE BRADEN,
author of *Tarot for Self Discovery*

# TAROT DECODED

# TAROT
# DECODED

**Understanding and Using Dignities and Correspondences**

## ELIZABETH HAZEL

Boston, MA/York Beach, ME

First published in 2004 by
Red Wheel/Weiser, LLC
York Beach, ME
With offices at:
368 Congress Street
Boston, MA 02210
*www.redwheelweiser.com*

**Library of Congress Cataloging-in-Publication Data**
Hazel, Elizabeth.
  Tarot decoded : understanding and using dignities and correspondences /
    Elizabeth Hazel.
        p. cm.
  Includes bibliographical references and index.
  ISBN 1-57863-302-8
    1. Hermetic Order of the Golden Dawn. 2. Tarot.  3. Dignities (Astrology).
BF1879.T2 H339 2004
133.3/2424 22                                        2003026031

Typeset in Minion by Sky-Peck Design
Printed in Canada
TCP

| 11 | 10 | 09 | 08 | 07 | 06 | 05 | 04 |
|----|----|----|----|----|----|----|----|
| 8  | 7  | 6  | 5  | 4  | 3  | 2  | 1  |

*This book is dedicated with gratitude
to Dr. Rilma Buckman—
teacher, mentor, friend, listener, and advocate.*

# CONTENTS

# ILLUSTRATIONS

# FOREWORD

**W**riting a book about tarot reading techniques is like dancing on a field of landmines. Very few areas of tarot history or methodology enjoy total agreement by tarot scholars, and diverse and conflicting opinions about praxis, symbolic content, attributions, kabbalistic associations, and whether other occult systems should be piggy-backed on to the tarot at all are the norm rather than the exception. A student progressing from beginner to intermediate stage soon encounters this quagmire of controversy. Students must know that although teachers and books may introduce them to the clout of diverse authorities on the subject of tarot, ultimately they must choose the type of tarot reading style and techniques that they will develop over time. Teachers provide the substance and tools, but the student must build a temple of stylistic method based on their own ability, discretion, and taste.

Dignities are imperative when tarot symbolism and divinatory meanings fall short of providing a cohesive interpretation of a card spread. There are two separate and intensely personal issues involved with dignities: the choice of techniques, and the choice of attribution systems. Generally the spectrum of techniques will grow and diversify over time, but the choice of attribution system may cause considerably more frustration. Tarot readers must test them, one by one, until they discover the system with which they have the best affinity (or until they discover that attribution systems are not for them). The kingdom of tarot is a democracy of one—pick your poison, and *abandon hope, all ye who enter here.*

The purpose of this book is not to insist that tarotists use the attribution system taught by the Hermetic Order of the Golden Dawn (which is presented here with minor modifications), but to provide guidelines and basic instructions for utilizing dignities of both occult and cartomantic origins. In order to present any instructions with believability, an author must take an authoritative tone. So I have chosen to write about what has proven effective for me after decades of working with tarot.

The search for a scientific explanation of the tarot is, in my view, a knee-jerk response to the contemporary zeitgeist obsessed with overweening rationalism, in effect beating God again and again to make sure he is really dead. Nothing would turn the living tarot into a desiccated corpse faster than prodding it into a scientific model of behavior. I prefer the mystique of limitless possibility that allows the tarot to function as a portal to the unknown.

Nevertheless, my preference for an unbounded tarot should not be confused with capitulation to mumbo-jumbo spiritualism or so-called clairvoyance. Quite the opposite, learning to interpret the tarot is a form of specialized intelligence that hones and facilitates the intuition. Without intellectual criteria for assessing card relationships, the intuition lacks a foundation of guidance and is prone to sloppy, inconsistent results. This is what dignity methods provide for the reader, and mastery of these techniques results in the presentation of seemingly other-worldly knowledge about a querent.

This book offers preliminary instructions in a complex subject. Ultimately, the readers of this book will select, on their own authority, the dignity techniques that enhance their ability to glean meaning and inspiration from the tarot. If this book assists tarotists in enhancing their interpretive abilities, it has fulfilled its mandate.

—EMH

# CHAPTER 1

# FORMS OF DIGNITY

*Kght 6 wands   P 9 S   Q of C*
      *Friendly        Neutral*

**D**ignity is the relationship between cards in a spread, and its analysis is a fundamental technique of tarot interpretation. A relationship between neighboring cards may be good, neutral, or bad, and it is determined by comparing attributions, elements, and numeric components and by analyzing for strength or weakness, assistance or frustration. A card that enjoys friendly neighbors or is placed in a location suitable to its attributes is in *good dignity, well-placed,* or *well-dignified,* and occasionally may gain the status of *perfect dignity.* Cards placed near neighbors that are neither friendly nor unfriendly may be considered in *neutral dignity.* If a card is surrounded by hostile neighbors, it is called *ill-dignified, debilitated, in detriment,* or *badly placed.*

Western occult tradition is built upon the philosophical ideas of the early Greeks, who devised a dignity system to judge and classify relationships between planets and zodiac signs. Many of the tarot terms that are used to describe dignity, therefore, are borrowed from identical or similar terms in astrology.

There are also forms of dignity specific to the tarot, generated by the numeric structure of the seventy-eight-card deck and the geometric dynamics of the spread form into which the cards are placed. The fifty-six cards of the Minor Arcana consist of four suits divided into four sets of Ace through Ten (forty pip cards); four sets of court cards (sixteen cards); and the twenty-two cards of the Major Arcana, usually numbered 0-XXI. The symbolism of tarot art has also been supplemented with attribution systems that usually include astrological relationships, elemental assignments, and alphabet and numeric associations. These attributions form a background that enriches meaning by inferring specialized relationships between particular cards.

Reversals—cards appearing upside-down in a spread—change the meaning of a card, but the attribution remains the same. In a reversed position, some card meanings may become less favorable, while others are improved. Since dignities express the nature of card relationships through attributions, a tarotist may view reversals as a peculiar or muted form of attribution, adapting the improved or deteriorated implications of a reversed card to the surrounding card dignities. Some tarotists who specialize in analyzing dignities do not use reversals at all, and the demonstrations in this book show all cards in an upright position.

European mystics like Falconnier, Papus, Wirth, Etteilla, and Levi created separate and unique sets of attributions to the tarot between 1780 and the late 1880s. These early systems are focused mostly on the trump cards. In the 1890s, a group called the Hermetic Order of the Golden Dawn taught a new group of tarot correspondences to their members, and this system is the one associated with the Waite-Smith deck and the Thoth deck. One advantage of the Golden Dawn attribution system is the detailed planetary and zodiacal assignments to the pip and court cards. This system is common to American and British tarotists (although certainly not unanimous), while Europeans often use the Continental attribution system, particularly with antique tarots like the Tarot de Marseilles. Various modern authors have created further original systems that are usually unique to a single deck. The Golden Dawn attribution system is used in this book as the basis for elemental and zodiacal dignity; the complete list of attributions is in appendix A.

## TYPES OF DIGNITY

There are several types of dignity that add to the spectrum of advanced forms of interpretation.

Elemental dignity is the most frequently mentioned usage and is based on assignments of the four elements, fire, water, air, and earth, to the four suits and trump cards. Elemental relationships provide basic clues to the interactions between neighboring cards. The elemental trumps—Fool, Hanged Man, Judgment, World—along with Aces and Pages (also called Princesses) have the virtues of pure elements, while the zodiacal trumps and pip cards share the element of their zodiacal attribution. Each level of status of the court cards (King, Queen, Knight, and Page or Princess)is also attributed to an element. Only the planetary trumps are free of elemental association, but they do experience affinities to certain elements. A significator card, the card that represents the querent in a reading, may be chosen by determining the querent's elemental traits.

**Modal dignity** may be conferred by any card with a zodiacal attribution. Modes are the *triplicity* of the zodiac; that is, the twelve signs are divided into three modes: *cardinal, fixed,* and *mutable.* A preponderance of a single mode in a spread gives emphasis to the specific energy type of that mode. Modes may also form sequences that suggest the direction of the energy flow between the card positions in a spread.

**Shared Status** is a specialized form of dignity for court cards, the sixteen cards designated by ascending royal titles. Court cards are assigned both element and mode. Shared status applies when sets (mode) or sequences (element) of court cards appear in a reading. For example, a set is a pair of Knights in a layout, and a small sequence the King and Queen of a single suit.

**Numeric dignity** occurs when sets and sequences appear in a spread. This form of analysis is specific to card reading and draws upon rules from poker and rummy, where points (or tricks) are dependent on matching number or suit groups. A set increases the influence of the numeric vibration, and one may use numerology or the rules of cartomancy (divining with playing cards) to interpret these groups. Sequences are comparable to a straight in poker—for example, Five, Six, Seven (regardless of suit). Sequences suggest a progression, or a process of development or deterioration that is occurring in the layout. Sets and sequences in tarot are more generalized than in card games—trumps and pips may be blended in sets; and cards of various suits may form numeric sequences. Cards may also share numeric dignity by being in a spread position of the same number, a form of dignity more properly belonging to the next category.

**Locational dignity** is related to an astrological concept called "accidental dignity," but is actually specific to tarot reading. It occurs when a card occupies a position in the spread that assists or undermines its strength and meaning. Spreads are usually organized into geometric forms that suggest favorable placements, both by the order of the card spread and by the position meanings. The astrological form of locational dignity may be applied to Cosmic Axis or Twelve-House spreads (described in chapter 9). These spread forms are derived from the horoscope house system and are related to the natural order of the zodiac. Locational dignity may be simple or infinitely complex.

**Planetary and Zodiacal dignities** are based on the particular system of attributions used with the tarot. In the Golden Dawn system, signs of the zodiac are attributed to twelve trump cards and are also assigned to court and pip cards. Planets are assigned to trump and pip cards on the basis of decan (ten-degree segments) rulership assignments. The traditional rules of astrological dignities govern the interrelationships between signs and planets assigned in the tarot. Although full use of astrological tarot attributions requires some knowledge of astrology to apply, it's also the method that allows the tarot to mimic the scope and accuracy of astrology. The Twelve-House spread is stretched to its full potential by blending the conventions of both tarot and astrology.

· · ·

Attributions and dignities don't change the divinatory meanings of the cards, or even specific deck-related meanings. By giving details to neighborly relationships, dignities add color and depth to the meaning of a card and provide underlying associations that define combinations and zones of emphasis (neighborhoods) in a spread. Dignities don't so much change a card's meaning as fine-tune it, as its neighbors increase its potency or dilute its intentions. Some cards, by nature, are more permeable and translucent, while others are relentlessly dynamic and aggressive. Dignities provide a basis for comprehending why the Knight of Wands might pop a baseball through the Tower's window. And although the various attribution systems applied to the tarot are myriad, the basic techniques and astrological conventions for using them are not.

The view of dignities offered in this book is "astrologically correct." In other words, my explanation of the use of dignities does not contradict astrological conventions, particularly in regard to the planetary trumps. Instead, I utilize astrological conventions to extend and amplify tarot dignities and blend them with card-specific forms of dignity. Thus given, the tarotist who chooses to learn astrology (or the astrologer learning tarot) will not struggle with incongruous methods but may proceed with a helpful foundation in the concept of dignity.

Planets are assigned on basis of decan (ten-degree segments), rulership assignments,

# CHAPTER 2

# ELEMENTARY ELEMENTS

I n tarot, astrology, magic, and alchemy there are four primary elements that clothe the spirit of life. These are fire, water, air, and earth, and these basic components have been a core part of the fabric of the occult sciences for about two thousand years, since the days of Ptolemy, Aristotle, and Plato.

The ancients determined there was an underlying order to the structure of the universe, and these four elements were the basis for all life on earth, all things in existence. The elements were superimposed on the twelve zodiac constellations and later became part and parcel of magic and alchemy. Henry Cornelius Agrippa gave detailed lists of the things composed of elemental blends around 1500 CE. Eventually, the four elements were grafted into the tarot.

There is some dissension about which element belongs to which suit in the tarot, but the most commonly used assignments are:

Fire = Wands
Water = Cups
Swords = Air
Pentacles = Earth

This is the system worked out by the Secret Chiefs of the Hermetic Order of the Golden Dawn and used in the Waite-Smith tarot deck, as well as in the Crowley-Harris Thoth deck. Since these two decks are the basis for the bulk of modern tarot decks (although certainly not all), this given system of attributions is a good starting point.

The four elements are like a family:

Fire = Father

Water = Mother

Air = Son

Earth = Daughter

The elements have affinities and preferences and characteristic results when one is blended with another. Elements are constantly trying to influence one another, to blend in new and meaningful ways. This view is the one held by Agrippa, and it is often neglected in contemporary explanations of elemental dignities.

In the basic concept of elemental dignities, there are friendly, neutral, and unfriendly pairings of the elements:

| Friendly | Neutral | Unfriendly |
|---|---|---|
| fire and air | fire and earth | fire and water |
| water and earth | air and water | air and earth |

In this primitive schema, if a wand is sitting next to a cup, they are at cross-purposes, each weakening the other. But in practice (and in the view of Agrippa), elements are much more subtle and prone to more intermingling than the above outline permits. Elemental dignities should be regarded as a flexible dynamic between neighbors rather than a set of ironclad rules. Fire and water may be at odds, but that friction accounts for the driving power of steam. Challenging relationships promote learning and growth, whereas compatible, easy relationships may devolve into inertia. The inherent characteristics of each element give a basis for understanding how it will respond to any of the other three elements.

## FIRE

Fire is hot and dry, according to Aristotle, thought by many to be the primal element of the universe (the biblical version: "Let there be light."). Prometheus was kicked out of Olympus for bringing the secrets of fire to humanity. Fire embodies the descent of spirit into matter, the primordial spark of life. But on a more practical level, as Prometheus knew, fire was a key survival tool, allowing people to cook their food and warm their wigwams. Providing both heat and light, fire is a critical necessity, and understanding how to use it is a great boon to humanity and the development of civilization. Likewise, the fiery light and warmth provided by the Sun's fusion is necessary for life and growth on Earth.

Some of the less friendly aspects of fire occur when it isn't controlled or is in the wrong hands—devastating fires that destroy forests, homes, and books that are out of favor with the goon squad. Fire is also demanding, because it needs to be fed. If there's no more wood or other flammable substances around to burn, it gets mighty cold in the winter. Fire is the enemy of trees. The Sun's fiery heat, in excess, can cause droughts, deserts, and miserable wastelands.

Fire can be the element of last resort, too. The Russians burned Moscow to the ground to prevent Napoleon from capturing the city, and General Sherman burned Atlanta to hasten the end of the Civil War. This method of warfare even has a fiery name—"scorched earth" policy. The dropping of two atomic bombs on Japan topped them all, raising the devastation by fire to the potential destruction of the world.

Fire, like all the other elements, has a range of behaviors, some quite uncontrollable. The suit of Wands exhibits many of these faces. We see the torch that lights the darkness in the Ace, ambitions and enthusiasms sparked in the Two. The Three has signal fires and welcoming candles in the window. The Four has the home fires freshly lit, ready for warmth, cooking, and fellowship. The fires of ambition rage in the Five; the Olympic torches mark champions in the Six. In the Seven, we keep the fire stoked to keep predators from attacking. The fire dwindles to the unearthly glow of coals in the Eight and Nine, with the popping of sparks as the fire shrinks. The deepening shadows keep the watcher looking over his shoulder. By the Ten, the fuel is gone and the fire has died, and there is nothing left but ashes.

The Wand court cards have fiery personalities. The Page is the pure, infant flame, nurtured on kindling to an awakening glow. The Knight burns with energy and ambition; he's hot to trot and has a combustible temper to match. Fire is better managed by the Queen; she has all the fuel she needs and knows how much to use for the size of fire she needs. The King masters fire—he has bellows to make white heat, furnaces, torches, flashlights, flares, and maybe even fireworks for celebrations.

This suit is motivated and informed by fire. Fire requires devotion, diligence, loyalty, and caution. Carelessness in fiery matters can result in destruction, whether this means an untended fire that burns down a house or a hot temper out of control. Whether a survival tool or one of mass destruction, fire commands respect. The fire of a spotlight can mark human triumph, but an untimely light cast into the shadows can catch a person with his or her hand in the cookie jar. Fire is the glory of stardom, and the ignominy of notoriety. It's never dull, however. And once a fire dies, it's difficult to rekindle.

## WATER

There isn't enough paper and ink to describe all of the faces of water, the mother element. From the dripping of a leaky faucet to the roaring of the rapids of the Colorado River, water embodies the extremes of mood and size. The qualities of water are cold and moist.

Before being born into the light of the world, fetuses float in a dark world of fluid in a placenta. For nine months, this inky, solitary ocean is a private universe, quiet and undisturbed. We long for a return to this preternatural, undifferentiated water. Water moves and seeks; it travels and changes form. It is rain, river, and ocean. Each mood of water has a voice, gurgling in a fountain or bellowing like the incoming tide in the Bay of Fundy. Water can be fresh and clear, like the cold streams running down from a mountain; it can be muddy and murky like a polluted river. It can be turbulent, salty, and colored an angry teal, like the high seas, or a pure dazzling turquoise like Lake Maracaibo in Venezuela.

Water is the symbolic mother of all liquids—frothy beer, hydrochloric acid, India ink. Water is the basis for every soup, sauce, and salad dressing ever invented. Humans are mostly water, about 80 percent, which is ironic considering that the bladder is the first to go. Powdered ochre and minerals mixed with water and fat were the first paints, and the slapping rhythms of the waves gave voice to the first primitive drum beat.

Emotions and feelings are the stuff of water, with their panoply of range and intensity. Falling in love is like the magnificent Angel Falls, where water heedlessly drops hundreds of feet from a cliff into vernal rain forest. Sorrow is like stagnant marsh water, fraught with chartreuse scum and the drone of mosquitoes and gnats. Belonging to a family or a group is like a wide flowing river, carrying us to a destination.

Yet without a container—a glass, a bowl, river, or ocean bed—water dissipates. It sinks into the earth or evaporates into the atmosphere. A lack of water brings death to plant and animal life. Early civilizations were always located near a reliable source of fresh water. The valley between the Tigris and Euphrates Rivers is called the "cradle" of civilization, evidence of the nurturing capacity of water. Water moves in and out without warning. The Dead Sea is drying up quickly, but in 1996 the Mississippi River surpassed its levies and caused wholesale destruction from flooding.

Much like emotions, water can't really be managed. It can be acknowledged, guided, and understood; preserved and kept as clean as possible, but water is a tricky customer. The suit of Cups is a reflection of water, insomuch as a cup can contain it.

In the Ace, primordial waters overflow the rim of the cup, symbolizing the rush of the birthing waters, the source of the river, the delta pouring water into a lake or ocean. This is the receptive liquid animated by the Wand's sparks. In the Two, water first becomes aware of the other, giving love, companionship, courtship, and harmonious feelings of well-being. In the Three, the water gurgles and patters in a celebration of happiness, music, and art as the outflow of awareness is shared with others. In the Four, the water is a still pool for reflection, not yet stagnant but unmoving and undisturbed. Water becomes turbulent and unruly in the Five as feelings flood the stillness. Finally the water passes the rapids to become a healthy river in the Six. The river is big and deep enough to contain emotions, memories, and continuity between generations.

Water becomes uncertain in the Seven—perhaps it moves freely through the delta, but it could become stuck in murky pools, turn into quicksand or some other quagmire waiting to entrap the unwary. The merging of earth, water, and sky may lull one into a stupor. Flow ceases and water becomes stagnant in the Eight. Water is leaking into the boat and slipping through fingers at once. No container is adequate for water in the Eight, and control is shown for the pretense that it is. Emotions slide into dark waters, longing for the precious safety of the womb, yet are exiled to isolation. Fresh rains bring relief in the Nine, welcome after the cloying humidity of the bogs, or deathly dryness of the desert. The waters sparkle and laugh, joined again before moving to the vast ocean in the Ten. Life, for its momentary detour through differentiation, has come again to the point of unity, thus including the individual in a history of race, clan, name, honor, achievement, dysfunction, and illness that flows through the river of blood from generation to generation.

The court cards embody the feeling nature of water. The Page is a gentle spring, small but lively. The Knight rides the waters to get where he's going, whether he's lassoed a raging flood or is diving into deep hidden underwater caverns. His emotions run the gamut from tenderly romantic to a torrential outpour. The Queen is the steady river, anchoring her family in good times and bad, and she transmits from her ancestors the blood that flows through her children. The King has learned to skim the waves and read the water's moods. He understands the nature of water and has learned to move with, rather than against, the flow. Like the beaver, he knows what materials make the best dikes, bridges, dams, and thus boats. His vessels are seaworthy.

Water is the heart of the great mother, warm and nurturing or cold, violent, and devouring. Patient observation reveals the ways and moods of waters and the overlying order in these rhythms. Yet with water, one must always be as aware of what is behind as what lies ahead. As the passengers of the *Titanic* discovered to their sorrow, Neptune, god of the ocean, is implacable in his retribution for hubris. The sea keeps its most precious secrets hidden, guarded by the ancient Hindu serpent goddess, Naga Kanya. From surface to the unexplored depths, water is an alien realm to humans after birth. We can't live in it, only on or beside it, and that at our peril. Water is where the cradle of life is rocked, with all of the nurturing safety of the good mother, and all the devouring dangers of the dark mother.

## AIR

A whisper of wind says it's time to visit with Air. He is the son, hot and dry, sly and unpredictable. A true child of his volatile father, Fire, and his unknowable mother, Water, Air permeates, penetrates, eludes capture, and has pervasive yet invisible influence. Air is everywhere and nowhere at the same time, but it's valuable. On *Sesame Street,* a Muppet in a trench coat, dark glasses, and a fedora sold a jar of air to the Cookie Monster for five cents. We may be given spirit by fire, and our bodies may be mostly made of water, but it takes air to keep us alive. It's worth the nickel. From the life-giving breath of air comes the Word, the capacity for knowledge and exchange.

Air gives names to everything, and without names, descriptions, ideas, and concepts, human civilization would stall. We don't know who first created language, but what would we be without it? In the Sanskrit language, word is form, and *Om* is the perfect word. In the Vedic belief system, the word *Om* was the primordial progenitor of existence. The father and son are alike in many ways, which is why they have such an affinity with one another. Air shares similar volatile qualities with fire.

Moving air may be the cat's paw of a breeze on a dull, hot day or a blustering north wind that pulls leaves from the trees in autumn. The ancients imagined Aeolus as the king of the winds, with four minions for each compass direction. The north wind is cold and treacherous, the east wind refreshing and inspiring, the south wind warm and wistful, the west wind damp with rain clouds. Air carries the clouds and teases them into fantastic shapes that nudge the imagination as they slide across the sky. Air and sky are one, making a palette of blue, gray, periwinkle, and indigo.

Like water, air is always moving, always restless, never a dull moment. Just when you think the wind is steady and true, it changes directions, gusts and ripples, or stops altogether. Air is faithful because it's always there, but fickle because it always changes. Winds become deadly as hurricanes, tornadoes, and monsoons. The trade winds have names like El Niño, La Niña, and other monikers created by mariners and weathercasters. In breathing, the breath is named. Heavy breathing is something likely to be naughty, shallow breathing tends to happen when we're panicky or caught unawares. We request a moment to catch our breath when we need to think, which shows just how closely air, breath, and thinking are entwined.

Air is the natural element of thought. We need to breathe to speak, to expound on ideas, to tease a friend, to preach to the choir, to extemporize, even to lie through our teeth. To live is to take one's first breath; to die is to take one's final breath. Air is ticklish, delicate, warm, or frosty, and it occupies every container unless purposefully vacuumed from it. Yet air is not contained, not docile, not domesticated like the water that comes from the kitchen faucet. Air adds a character to every environment—the stuffy air of a basement, the processed air of an airplane, the vast air of the open plains, the cool morbid air of a morgue. Air is easy to take for granted, but it's persistently prevalent in almost every facet of life.

In the suit of Swords, Air rages to life in the Ace. It is the furious birth of the first idea, the initial concept, the innate intelligence of life itself. It's the wind that gives life to the battle horns, charging forward with fearless determination. In the Two, air is a tease, the twitching of a cat's whiskers or the flopping of doggie ears. It blows back and forth, whispering in one ear and then the other. In the Three, unexpected gusts blow papers down the street and the victim runs to recapture them, full of anxiety. In the Four, the winds are momentarily still, but this is an illusion. Even when the wind is still on the ground, the mind may rise to the gusts moving the tree branches. In the Five, all hell breaks loose as air tugs, pushes, blusters, and howls. This is the wind that carries the violent storm, compelling one to batten down the hatches and sit it out in some pathetic corner of safety. The Big Bad Wolf manages to blow down the first two pigs' houses until the third figures out how to build one of brick in the Six. The Six's air is the perfect breeze that fills the sails. It lubricates the mind, carrying the scent of hope and the sound of satisfied laughter. In the Seven, the wind becomes elusive and taunting. This is the wind that can't be defined, captured, or contained. It's the pesky buzz of a fly you can hear but can't see. Air is the enemy in the Eight. It surrounds and entraps. From north, east, south, west, it presses relentlessly, implacable and possibly deadly. The air crumbles all defenses in the Nine. Words are pretentious at this point, and the ideas that sounded so good in the earlier versions become like buzzards plucking at flesh. The air is full of bacteria, viruses, parasites, and a host of unseen threats. Barriers are futile in the Ten. The wind has died, the thoughts are silenced, and words have lost all of their power. This air is deathly still, the quiet of the field after a battle, where only the ghosts of the fallen have anything to say.

In the court cards, air demonstrates its many facets. The Page is quick-witted, sharp-tongued, elusive, and slightly wicked. The weathervane spins and totters in its efforts to point which way her thoughts are turning. The Knight partakes of the danger of the air—the killing winds of destruction that batter and torment. He takes ruthless satisfaction in shredding theories and suggestions but can be equally charming and witty when he proposes an idea. The Queen is the mistress of the intellect, her sails open to catch the wind to her advantage. She commands the force and direction of the airs and dances on the breezes with abandon when she is pleased. The King rides the winds and knows its creatures—the birds, the insects, even the puffs of milkweed floating in sunlight. He directs his thoughts like fighter planes and can be a kamikaze intellectual, silencing the proposals of his opponents in a courtroom. His arguments are sound, his logic impeccable, his inner thoughts impenetrable. He speaks when he has something to say and engages in trivialities when it amuses him. Such is the master of the winds.

## EARTH

Earth is the daughter, perfect of form, a manifestation of love and substance, and life is a tribute to her abundance and diversity. Earth is the most real, the most substantive element of the four, with the qualities of dry and cold. Because she is the essence of form, earth is the source of life's greatest sorrows and pleasures. Spirit is incarnated into a body, and this body experiences the world. In youth, bodies are pliable, strong, and a source of pleasure. In old age, bodies remind us of mortality with aches, pains, limitations. At death, we shed our bodies to return to the stars, opening the ziplock baggie of incarnation.

Earth is profuse, abundant, diverse, vast, and incomparable. She is the awesome majesty of a mountain range, the tiny universe contained in a faceted emerald. Her body is all greens and browns, but in warmer seasons she is clothed in the fabulous riot of floral color. Earth is the reddest rose, the pinkest lily, the whitest hyacinth. She's the rainbow's body, basking under the glowing sun as her trees reach to the sky. She keeps secret beauty in hidden caves full of crystals, gold, and precious minerals.

Earth is inclined to be still and placid but may shake and tremble, and vomit searing magma from a volcano. In her quaking fury, no creatures are safe. Every feature of her surface is a feast for the eyes—the forest, the meadow, the plowed fields, the rolling hills, the canyons, cliffs, and plateaus. Maps describe terrains by showing varying surface features. Yet from outside its atmosphere, Earth is a blue and white orb, floating in the lonely blackness of space and time.

Earth is the element that is the embodiment of life, because life requires form for existence. Life is everything from tiny microorganisms to vistas of land, yet the common thread is manifestation into form. Without form, ideas are a chimera, unreal and unmanifested. Earth is the difference between something and nothing. In the scheme of elements, fire and water have vast powers, and air is their natural beneficiary. But earth, the daughter, is the end result of all of their movements. She gives form for their survival and determines the longevity of each form; she is the substance of time.

Earth changes, but slowly. Hers are not the cagey movements of air and fire, or the slippery stealth of water, but the slow development of each thing from birth to maturity to death. Her forms are always in a state of transition in this respect, but these phases overlap so that form and life are continuous events. This is the chain of life, the double helix of DNA, the spiral of time as it manifests in form. She's the most humble, the most quiet, but the most crucial as well.

The suit of Pentacles is one of material properties, and it focuses on the cycles of birth, development, and erosion to which form is subjected. The Ace is the birth of form, the perfected child of the other three elements manifested [Earth] into raw existence. Identity is derived from form, and reality from substance. In the Two, emerging forms discover that isolation isn't possible. New forms compete to acquire a foundation and sustenance for their ultimate maturation. Needs and desires manifest in this naive reality, but fulfillment is distant. In the Three, earth gains an initial level of mastery of form. Ideas gain substance through industry and drive ambitions for further development in the world. The earth of the Three is responsive and fertile, while at the Four, earth becomes responsible as it accumulates wealth and reputation. Here earth is a well-established foundation for future growth. Fire, water, and air are amalgamated in form-giving earth, and this is a great achievement. In the Five, earth realizes the potential for deterioration. Now it's worried and anxious—it can't protect everything, nor can it fulfill every desire and need. The reality of form has to be prioritized. But fertility and possibility return in the Six. Earth enjoys the luxury of pleasure, as she yields her secret buried metals and gems, fodder for the clever smith. Here earth is the palette of the craftsman, the stuff of every beautiful object. Humans fashion the products of earth's body into treasures and heirlooms, gardens and homes.

In the Seven, earth's defenses are eroded. It is uncertain, insecure, and prone to aching knees and squeaky hinges. Time has taken a toll, and some of earth's features need repair, attention, remaking. The Eight provides this attention, fixing broken items, remaking old forms into new ones. Quiet concentration is necessary at this stage. While nothing lasts forever, life and form can be extended with careful stewardship. In the Nine, earth reaches perfection, as all the details of form coalesce into beauty. The expressive power of art transcends the substance of its media. The Ten is the final result of manifestation, and earth is transformed into monuments that belong to all and survive through countless generations. These are the forms that are inherited and maintained through time. The family estate, the structure of facial bones, the texture of hair, and even the ghost in the family closet belong to the Ten. This is the deathless Ten, the substance that remains though mortals die. It's the collective mark on earth that humanity makes by building, developing, and laboring to construct on the path of time's spiral. The individual adds to this legacy with a lifetime's work. This Ten gives hope for tomorrow as no other card can.

The court cards embody different aspects of relating to form and substance. The Page learns and absorbs the nature of reality; she is a student of lore, history, and technique. She knows the value of dedicated labor and the rewards of play after labor. The Knight is steady and determined, his hand on the plow, his back and legs giving momentum against the earthy substance he's trying to manage and tame. He plants and cultivates, and then waits patiently for results. No wild rider is this Knight; he knows what he wants and plots to obtain it. The Queen is docile, patient, and clever, tending her family's needs and working efficiently to manage their goods and properties. She is clever in acquisition and nurtures all that she meets with an eye toward growth and maturity. Her dealings are sound and realistic, because she wants to retire in comfort rather than poverty. The King is the master of earth and leaves his mark through building, creating, and ownership. He forms channels through which wealth flows into his control, and he is patient with development but impatient with foolishness and waste. He is eminently practical and pragmatic, and respected for his ability to accumulate and diversify.

• • •

And so the tour through the elements ends. The elements are completely simple, yet ultimately complex and intertwined. Affinities are secondary to their natural mandate to relate and blend with one another. Pure examples of the elements are rare, and an infinite multitude of combinations is displayed in varying degrees and differing measures. The four elements are subject to family dynamics, as the father, mother, son, and daughter relate and respond to one another. Each family member fulfills a role in the group and will act in a manner that is described by the specialized setting shown by the card and its neighbors. The court cards are a microcosm of the elements, a miniature laboratory of elemental family dynamics. The elemental trumps convey the archetypal qualities of elements, while the pip cards show the composition of settings and conditions surrounding the querent. Understanding elements in their purity is to begin the journey of understanding elements in their combined diversity.

Pip = show settings +
conditions

# CHAPTER 3

# ELEMENTAL COURT CARDS

C ourt cards display a special aspect of elements, as they show the humanized, personified characteristics and maturation process of each element. Each element is developed, by age and gender, as it moves through the four status levels of the court cards, from the Page (or Princess) to the King. The court cards provide a unique repository of dignities, because they convey elements, modes, sets and sequences, and status in a way that is particular to the human species. The specialized blend of dignities exchanged by the court cards is herein termed *shared status.*[1]

Each level of courtly status is assigned to an element in addition to the suit's element. The Kings (father) embody the element of fire. The Queens (mother) are the element of water. The Knights (son) are the element of air, and the Pages or Princesses (daughter) are the element of earth. The Princess of Pentacles, the Knight of Swords, the Queen of Cups, and the King of Wands have the virtue of identical suit and status element—earth of earth, air of air, water of water, and fire of fire respectively—and are the purest representatives of their suit and element.

In astrological analysis, each individual's birth chart presents a blend of varying elemental, modal, and planetary factors that are interpreted by

---

1 The concept of status in the human species is discussed in Desmond Morris, *The Human Zoo* (New York: McGraw-Hill, 1969), pp. 41-78. Morris, an anthropologist, makes revealing observations about the motives and drive for status in humans and other animal species. The court cards of the tarot are, of course, designated by royal appellations, so the acquisition of status is implied by the titles given to these sixteen cards. Jung also notes the prevalence of royal status in many myths and fairy tales, and equates this construction with the drive for individuation—that is, the quest to rule one's own existence in a state of wholeness (see Carl Jung, "The Phenomenology of the Spirit in Fairytales," in *The Archetypes and the Collective Unconscious* (Princeton: Princeton Univ. Press, 1969), pp. 207-55).

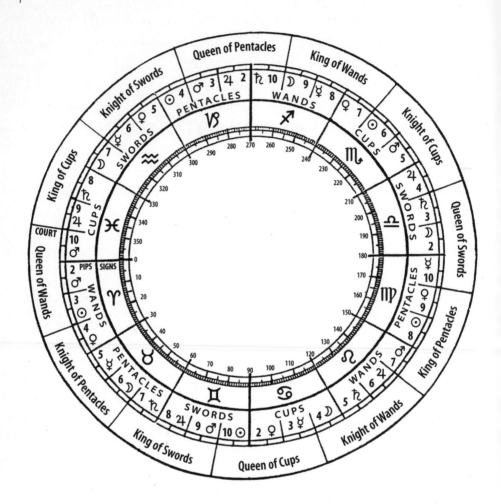

*Figure 1: Horoscope Diagram of Court Card Attributions*

placement and dignity. The Golden Dawn system utilizes all the 360 degrees of the zodiac for the court cards and assigns the twelve zodiacal cusps to the Knights, Queens, and Kings. The Princesses aren't mature enough to own zodiacal property but are in the process of learning to serve the other cards (see figure 1). The cusps include the final ten degrees of one sign and the first twenty degrees of the next sign. The second sign is of greater importance and matches the element of the suit. It's more succinct (and less complex for non-astrologers) to express these attributions as cusps, tacitly emphasizing the sign that relates to the suit's element. The Queens are attributed to the cardinal cusps of their element; the Knights to the fixed-sign cusps; and the Kings to mutable-sign cusps (see table 1).

The attributions to the Kings and Knights may be reversed, with the Kings as fixed signs and the Knights as mutable signs. Confusion about these attributions result from the status changes applied to these cards by Golden Dawn members. In MacGregor Mather's *Book T* (1871), the old Knight becomes the new King, and the new Prince is the old King. Similarly, in Crowley's *Book of Thoth* (1944) and Thoth deck, the King was renamed the Knight (old king relinquishing control) and the Knight was renamed the Prince (new king coming into power). These status flip-flops and subliminal references to the Fisher King legend are fine for those who are dedicated to the Golden Dawn's legacy, but very few decks actually utilize these title changes for the King and Knight. Consequently, I have found the straightforward family and modality relationships to be the most compelling, with the Kings as the fathers who germinate the next generation (mutable) and the Knights as sons who require fastness of purpose and single-minded intensity to gain their ends (fixed).

Joined with the keywords of their modal content, the Queens *conceive* (cardinal); the Knights *develop* (fixed); and the Kings *transcend and fertilize*

## Table 1: Court Card Attributions by Zodiac Sign

|  | Queens (Cardinal) | Knights (Fixed) | Kings (Mutable) |
|---|---|---|---|
| WANDS | Pisces/**Aries** | Cancer/**Leo** | Scorpio/**Sagittarius** |
| CUPS | Gemini/**Cancer** | Libra/**Scorpio** | Aquarius/**Pisces** |
| SWORDS | Virgo/**Libra** | Capricorn/**Aquarius** | Taurus/**Gemini** |
| PENTACLES | Sagittarius/**Capricorn** | Aries/**Taurus** | Leo/**Virgo** |

Table 2: The Court Card Keywords and Dignities

| Mode & Element | Infant Element (Earth) Princesses | Fixed (Air) Knights | Cardinal (Water) Queens | Mutable (Fire) Kings |
|---|---|---|---|---|
| **Wands** Fire | Ignition | Combustion | Application | **Illumination** |
| **Cups** Water | Reflection | Turbulence | **Immersion** | Buoyancy |
| **Swords** Air | Inception | **Invention** | Transmission | Refinement |
| **Pentacles** Earth | **Conception** | Dedication | Manifestation | Embodiment |

(mutable). The Princesses are an infant form of each element manifesting in earth, immature but vital, with great potential for growth. As such, the Princesses are closely related to the Aces and the elemental trumps.

In order to better understand the idea of elements and modes with the court cards, table 2 shows keywords for each of the court cards. These keywords can be augmented with other terms; the table is a starting point for grasping the concept. A sixteen-court-card spread based on this table demonstrates how the humanized elements assume roles and display personality types (see figure 2 on page 28).

## SIGNIFICATORS

Before we look at the court card spread we should examine the card that represents the querent, which is called a *significator card*. The sixteen court cards are the primary repository of personality types in the tarot. Yet individuals often display multiple and contradictory characteristics and behaviors. This isn't surprising, as the vast spectrum of humanity can hardly be limited to sixteen modes of expression. In astrology, a birth horoscope (natal chart) is drawn using the whole circle of the zodiac. The Ascendant and houses and location of the Sun, Moon, and the planets are a myriad of factors that symbolically delineate the personality. In a tarot spread, neighboring pip cards serve to detail the court cards' personalities, motivations, actions, and environment. Trump cards display the overlying influences that a court card is subject to, showing issues or conditions of necessity that the court card must encounter.

The simplest method of choosing a significator card is to match the querent's Sun sign, gender, and/or age group with a court card. An older Pisces gentleman corresponds to the King of Cups, while a young college student, a Leo, may correspond to either the Knight or Princess of Wands. A person under the age of eighteen will usually be assigned to one of the Princesses. Often this is a satisfactory method for selecting a significator. On occasion, conflicting factors make a Sun-sign significator inappropriate. The current state of the querent's development may contradict age or gender factors. Elemental and modal blending is the stuff of the correspondence between the querent and the significator card chosen for that querent.

Carl Jung's theory of four personality types and their functions [2] may be corresponded with the four elements of the tarot suits, and this is a good starting point for choosing a significator. The fiery court cards are creative and ambitious, thus relating to Jung's *intuiting* function. The watery court cards are sensitive and deeply emotional, thus relate to *feeling*. The airy Swords court cards are intellectual and swift of tongue, therefore relating to the function of *thinking*. Finally, the earthy Pentacle court cards are dedicated and practical, thus allied with the function of *sensing*. These elemental personality functions are further subdivided by maturity and development, building the status in the royal order of the four court cards of each suit.

Jung's four functioning types operate together in the composition of a personality. There is always a single, predominant function evident in a personality, and two that are evident but of lesser importance. The fourth function is contained in the unconscious. In choosing a tarot significator with Jung's functioning types in mind, the tarotist will need to select the

---

2 Jung's exposition on personality types is presented in "Psychological Types," in *The Portable Jung*, ed. Joseph Campbell, (New York: Penguin Books, 1971), 178-269.

dominant personality function—the elemental (suit) component. The secondary function will convey the status of the querent, or may be of sufficient current importance to adjust the suit chosen.

Once ascertained, these functions can be related to the cusps or elemental blends indicated by the court card attributions. For example, if a young man is energetic and ambitious but is concerned about a love relationship, this implies an *intuiting* person with *feeling* concerns. The primary personality characteristic is fiery (by suit—Wands, by status—King), and the subordinate characteristic equates with water (by suit—Cups, by status—Queen). The water/fire cusps are owned by the Wand court cards, and the reader may select either the Knight or King of Wands, depending upon the age of the querent, or by determining whether the querent is involved in a process of development (fixed Knight) or more oriented to gaining mastery in his relationship (mutable King). The Knight of Cups may also be selected (a young man concerned about a watery issue), or the Queen of Wands (fiery suit with watery status).

Significators are not required for every spread, so the use of significator cards is at the discretion of the tarotist. In the course of a lifetime, individuals may correlate to various court cards. Although a person may identify with one court card above all others, time may modify this relationship, or the person may find him- or herself playing other roles that correspond more accurately to other court cards. Therefore, the idea of a significator card should be imbued with flexibility, as the overall personality of the querent merges with his or her current role of greatest importance.

When the significator card isn't withdrawn from the deck, the tarotist may silently choose it and seek it in the querent's spread. If it appears, the surrounding cards will describe the conditions around the querent and may also provide specific direction for seeking future assistance if needed. Other factors that may be revealed are health or mental focus and the condition of relationships, finances, ambitions, and worries. In this way, the significator card may actually be of more use when it's included in the deck. Another option for keeping the significator card in the deck is to simply select the significator card from a second deck, thus leaving the first deck intact.

## THE COURT CARD SPREAD

Separate the sixteen court cards from the deck and choose a significator card to represent yourself or a querent. The card may be chosen to represent the self-view or may reflect a role being played in a current situation. Shuffle the sixteen cards and place them face down in the order shown in figure 2 on page 28. All of the court cards are used.

Turn up the cards, row by row. Note the location where the significator card appears. Compare the significator card's keyword to the keyword of its position using the court card grid in table 2. Determine dignity by assessing the position: Has the significator card appeared in its own element/suit? Does it appear in a position of its own mode/status (i.e., a Queen in the Queen row)? If not in its own element/suit row, does this card appear in a row that is friendly, neutral, or unfriendly by element? Does the keyword that belongs to the significator card blend or clash with the keyword for the position where it has fallen? Has the significator card moved up in status (encountering new challenges) or moved down in status (needing to relearn a lesson)? Does this change in mode—if there is one—suggest greater or lesser effort on the part of the querent, or a change of attitude? What does the significator card learn in its position in the spread? Are its immediate neighbors friendly or hostile?

Here is a sample interpretation. The querent has chosen the Queen of Cups (Immersion) as the significator card, and it appears in the King of Swords position (12—Refinement). The querent has a nurturing and loving persona (cardinal water qualities) that others may experience as incisive, inspiring and capable of clever multitasking (mutable air qualities). The rise in status implies that the querent may need to play the role of the King, reaching for a more intellectual and masterful approach to the current situation by accessing the airy part of her nature to supplement the watery side. Water and air are neutral, uniting with a bit of effort. A logical viewpoint or detached attitude may require conscious effort, but it isn't excessively difficult. The cardinal Queen diversifies into the mutable King and may exert mastery by refining her ideas and thoughts with clarity and purpose. Clearly, the querent

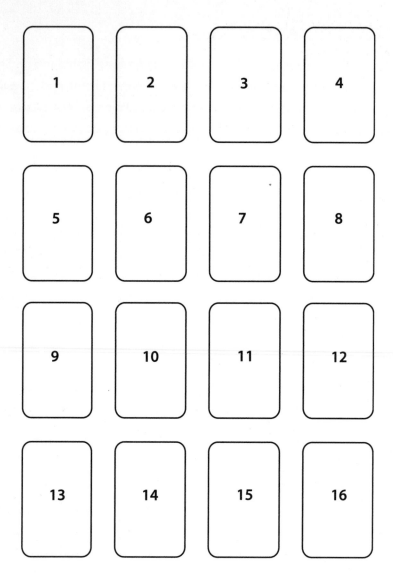

*Figure 2: Court Card Spread*

## Court Card Spread Comparisons

### First row—Fire element

1. _____ to Princess of Wands; _____ to Ignition
2. _____ to Knight of Wands; _____ to Combustion
3. _____ to Queen of Wands; _____ to Application
4. _____ to **King of Wands**; _____ to Illumination

### Second row—Water element

5. _____ to Princess of Cups; _____ to Reflection
6. _____ to Knight of Cups; _____ to Turbulence
7. _____ to **Queen of Cups**; _____ to Immersion
8. _____ to King of Cups; _____ to Buoyancy

### Third row—Air element

9. _____ to Princess of Swords; _____ to Inception
10. _____ to **Knight of Swords**; _____ to Invention
11. _____ to Queen of Swords; _____ to Transmission
12. _____ to King of Swords; _____ to Refinement

### Fourth row—Earth element

13. _____ to **Princess of Pentacles**; _____ to Conception
14. _____ to Knight of Pentacles_____ to Development
15. _____ to Queen of Pentacles_____ to Manifestation
16. _____ to King of Pentacles_____ to Embodiment

is currently advised to attend to the tasks of managing the situations in her life, rather than conceiving and initiating new projects.

When the dignity of the significator card has been thoroughly examined, compare the remaining card-to-position keywords. Evaluate whether the roles or personality factors in life assist or debilitate the querent. Some roles are easier than others. Each of the sixteen card placements may be given dignity analysis in terms of element, status, mode, and meaning, and by comparing keywords.

Let's look at another sample. If the Princess of Cups appears in the Princess of Wands position (1), the terms are expressed thus: *Reflection to Ignition*. There is an affinity of status here, because a Princess has appeared in a Princess position. But elementally, water and fire are opposites. The terms show this conflict—ignition is an active and spontaneous event, while reflection is a passive state. The Princess of Cups is the operative card here, so it suggests a time of reflection on beginnings, thus modifying the spontaneous quality of fire with the gentle and observant qualities of water. The first row speaks to the creative aspect of life and should be related to the birth or infancy (Princess) of the querent's personal goals.

After the individual cards are examined for dignity, the spread may be analyzed as a whole. Consider the roles of the elements in each of the horizontal rows. The top row, the element of fire, describes creativity, ambitions, and the dynamics of self-interest. The second row, the element of water, is invested in relationships and influenced by emotions. The third row, the element of air, is engaged in interpersonal communication, the exchange of attitudes, opinions, and facts. The fourth row, the element of earth, represents the practical, security-oriented efforts of the querent. Evaluate which horizontal rows are occupied by the most comfortable cards, according to status (mode) and elemental dignity. Scrutinize carefully the rows whose occupants struggle by status and dignity. Ill-dignified rows are areas of life where the querent needs to consciously focus and better understand personal strengths or weaknesses— or the elemental qualities requiring extra effort to express productively.

The vertical rows, showing the court card status/mode, may be evaluated in the same manner. The higher the court card's status, the more mature is the personified action of the element. For example, if the Princess of Pentacles falls in the King of Cup's position, there is a challenge for the Princess—*Conception to Buoyancy.* This card-to-position combination suggests an effort to evaluate the birth, or the genesis (earthy Princess), of the querent's emotional conclusions (watery King).

It should also be noted that the Princess of Pentacles is a double-element card, earth of earth. The four double-element cards should receive special attention regarding their placement; and similarly, compare the cards that occupy these four positions (4, 7, 10, and 13). The four double-element court cards are the most typical representatives of their element, so their designated positions require the most elementally relevant, true-to-form effort.

This spread fulfills a twofold purpose: it provides a contained exercise for dignity analysis through the restricted use of sixteen court cards (both the spread and the cards have a clear set of dignities); and it serves as an exercise for ascertaining and understanding the roles that one plays in life. The form on page 29 simplifies the process of comparison. Fill in the names of the cards drawn for each row and their keywords as they fall in the positions of the spread. The double-element court cards are highlighted.

This spread can be modified to analyze a relationship. A significator is chosen for the querent, and a second significator chosen for the significant other (lover, spouse, boss, friend, relative, etc.). The positions of the two significators in the spread are analyzed for strengths and weaknesses. If the significators chosen are different by element or status, the contrasting element and status rows of the two significator cards should receive special analysis to determine dignity.

From this exercise, it's easy to see the vivid relationships between the court cards. When utilizing a complete deck, the various aspects of element, mode, and status provided by the court cards should be examined as they relate to trumps and pips. Court cards may form sets or sequences by status or element, and both are instances of shared status. A rare incident of shared status occurs when all four court cards of a suit appear (a royal flush in poker), conveying the full potency of the personified element and a complete expression of developed status. A progression of shared status moving upward (i.e., from Knight to King) indicates growing mastery and understanding, or may suggest that an individual in the querent's life is becoming more important. A regression of status, from King to Knight, indicates a need to relearn lessons, to modify the flow of modal energies in current situations, or to reassess or diminish another's influence in a situation.

Since twelve court cards are assigned to thirty degrees of zodiacal arc (three decans) in the OGD system, they have a special relationship with the three pip cards that belong to their assigned decans. The Queens are assigned to Tens, Twos, and Threes; the Knights to Fours, Fives, and Sixes; and the Kings to Sevens, Eights, and Nines.

Here's an example. The Queen of Wands is assigned to 21° Pisces-20° Aries, so her territory of rulership includes the Ten of Cups (Mars/final decan of Pisces), the Two of Wands (Mars/first decan of Aries), and the Three of Wands (Sun/second decan of Aries). Since the Queen is one-third mutable and two-thirds cardinal by attribution, this gives her one mutable and two cardinal pip cards. These are the cards for her cusp, and when they appear near her in a spread are enlivened and strengthened to the most characteristic expression of their divinatory meaning. Figure 1 in this chapter and the horoscope diagram in appendix F provide a graphic display of the court cards and their related pip cards for further study.

# CHAPTER 4

# MODAL DIGNITIES

**W**hat is modality? In astrology, the twelve zodiac signs are divided into four elements, resulting in three signs (a trinity) of each element. The twelve signs are also organized into three modes with four signs in each modality (a quaternity).

The three-fold division consists of:

> **Cardinal signs:** Aries, Cancer, Libra, Capricorn

> **Fixed signs:** Taurus, Leo, Scorpio, Aquarius

> **Mutable signs:** Gemini, Virgo, Sagittarius, Pisces

Elements show the compositional property of each sign and card, or *of what they are made.* The modes show the quality of the elemental property, or *how the element is likely to behave.*

## THE MODES

### Cardinal Signs

Cardinal signs are feisty, charge-ahead, vigorous signs. Their keynote quality is their *capacity to conceive and give birth.* This mode is represented by the zodiacal attributions to the Queens, who own the four solstice and equinox cusps.

**Aries:** fire conceives identity, idealism, and quests.

**Cancer**: water conceives family growth, domestic stability, and motherhood.

**Libra**: air conceives primary communication, codes of behavior, ethics, and formal relationship agreements between people, such as marriage and business partnerships.

**Capricorn**: earth conceives material foundations, hierarchies, ownership, leadership, and parenting.

Cardinal signs courageously accept risks and are skilled at promoting their reputation and pet projects to others. The challenge is the potential for bullying, impatience, and shocked outrage when others fail to fall into step with their latest idea. Cardinal signs tend to assess loyalty in terms of validation, confirmed when others see their achievements in a positive manner and willingly support their goals. Cardinal signs are the sprinters, the signs moving most quickly to the next opportunity. Yet they may be winded by the time the goal is in sight, or the goal may lose their interest if not quickly obtained.

## Fixed Signs

Fixed signs are moderate, sensibly paced, dedicated, and determined. Their keynote quality is their *capacity to grow and evolve*. Fixed signs are given by zodiacal attribution to the Knights.

**Taurus**: earth is dedicated to accumulation, endurance, and longevity.

**Leo**: fire is devoted to the development of unique personal identity, the mastery of talents and passions, and to love and friendship.

**Scorpio**: water develops the trust and mutuality required to give tenacity to Libra's agreements, and it embodies the persistent evolutionary demand for procreation.

**Aquarius**: air develops the sciences and social organizations, and shapes the desired results that give power to Capricorn's leadership.

The fixed signs are "power" signs, able to nurture and bring to flower the original material provided by the cardinal signs. Fixed signs are cautious and slow-moving, yet paradoxically capable of remorseless change when the substances at hand fail to perform and patience wears thin. The fixed modality's weakness is a stubborn resistance toward change in the face of encroaching obsolescence. Issues about trust run through all the fixed signs. The basis for power and influence is acquired through patiently developed trust and loyalty. The fixed signs conduct prudent evaluations on the ability of others to follow through on their promises. Insecurity and fear of lack is at the root of the fixed-sign tendency toward greed and gluttony. These signs gain clues about ethics, humor, and communication from airy or mutable factors, and this will often determine if the need to develop is motivated by inspiration, fear, envy, humanitarian causes, or mere plodding labor for security.

## Mutable Signs

The Mutable signs are flexible and adaptable, and they represent both the final modality and the preparation of each element to be reborn in cardinal form. As such, their keynote quality is the *capacity to transform and fertilize.* The mutable signs are attributed to the Kings. These signs embody a deeply spiritual constitution, as they represent the highest and lowest final manifestation of each element.

**Gemini:** air rejoices in the diversity of life and the flexibility of communication; it elaborates on the inventive fruits of Aquarius and expands the social network initiated by Libra.

**Virgo:** earth coordinates the need to purify and transcend the foundations and leadership of Capricorn and manages the accumulated wealth of Taurus for the benefit of family and community.

**Sagittarius:** fire envisions the need for an elevated perspective of the raw, dynamic vision of Aries and a universal application of the individualization of Leo.

**Pisces:** water desires the return to the vast cosmic ocean, from which life was conceived in Cancer. Pisces inspires the bonding power of love that romanticizes the sexual and reproductive drives of Scorpio and the compassionate liturgies of religious tradition that confer sacredness to birth, marriage, and death.

The mutable signs tend to be the diplomats of the zodiac, because they are seldom irrevocably invested in a particular outcome. This allows these signs to view the big picture of their particular element in a visionary, conceptual, or ideological manner. Mutable signs have a singular talent for analyzing situations, for quick responses, and for being able to sum up complex ideas in a simple form. These signs are rarely judgmental and adopt a "live and let live" policy toward others. The challenge of mutable signs is found in the excess of unconcern. They can be too easygoing, letting life slip through their fingers through a lack of applying their efforts to a single goal. Mutable signs make great efforts to please others, only to find they have done themselves a disservice by jettisoning their powers of choice to the cardinal and fixed signs. These signs are often given a bounty of great talent but must focus to carry these gifts to their fruition.

## MODALITY IN THE TAROT

The pip cards have their modal assignments in this order:

**Twos, Threes, and Fours** of all suits are cardinal.

**Fives, Sixes, and Sevens** of all suits are fixed.

**Eights, Nines, and Tens** of all suits are mutable.

The court cards are also organized by modes:

**Queens:** 21° mutable sign through 20° cardinal sign, capacity to conceive.

**Knights:** 21° cardinal sign through 20° fixed sign, capacity to grow.

**Kings:** 21° fixed sign through 20° mutable sign, capacity to seed next cycle.

Zodiacal trump cards can also be organized by modes according to their attributions:

| Cardinal | Fixed | Mutable |
|----------|-------|---------|
| Emperor [♈] | Hierophant [♉] | Lovers [♊] |
| Chariot [♋] | Strength [♌] | Hermit [♍] |
| Justice [♎] | Death [♏] | Temperance [♐] |
| Devil [♑] | Star [♒] | Moon [♓] |

The elemental trumps—Fool (air), Hanged Man (water), Judgment (fire), World (earth)—don't fit into modalities. They embody the idea of pure elements, as do the Aces and Princesses. Elemental trumps, Aces, and Princesses absorb, reflect, and influence neighboring cards and derive modality from their neighbors. For instance, the Six of Wands may comfortably share its fixed-fire (Leo) mode when placed next to the Page of Wands. The planetary trumps supercede both elemental and modal dignities.

## USING MODAL DIGNITIES

### Example 1

This reading is for a client—let's call him Bob. Bob wants to know if the business venture he's considering will be successful. Figure 3 on page 38 shows the cards that appeared in a Cosmic Axis spread (see chapter 9 for further details on this spread).

Bob got his reading in the autumn, while the Sun was in Libra; he is Aquarian by birth.

The first two cards are cardinal. This shows enormous drive, ambition, and vigor being applied to his enterprise. Bob has done some legwork in the community (Three of Wands) and is fully obsessed with his goals for the future (Devil). The Eight of Cups reveals some glitches. First, this is a mutable card and shows that some of the material resources that Bob needs, possibly cooperation from government or business associates (Devil), may be elusive.

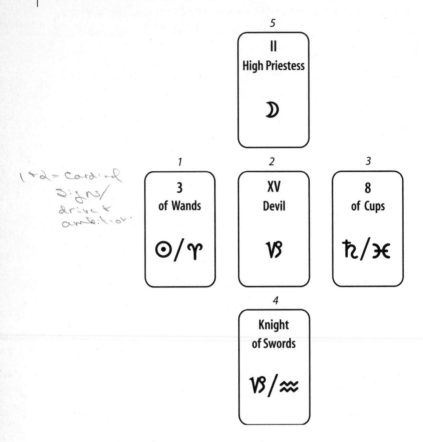

1+2 = cardinal signs/ drive + ambition.

*Figure 3: Bob's Reading*

Order of card placement, position meaning, and modality are:

1. The Individual: Three of Wands; cardinal

2. Current Perspective/Central Idea: XV the Devil; cardinal

3. The Other: Eight of Cups; mutable

4. Foundation or Past of the Issue: Knight of Swords; fixed

5. The Future: II the High Priestess; Moon; no mode or element

and hard to acquire at this time. He may also find this enterprise disrupts his relationships with loved ones; or crucial business contacts may be at a distance and unavailable to help.

The fourth card is the Knight of Swords, an appropriate significator card for Bob. Bob has leadership ability (cardinal Capricorn) and a good idea that he feels can be developed (fixed Aquarius). The fixed sign dominates this card, giving Bob the tenacity to stick with his plans and expand them further. He's a natural communicator (an Aquarius Sun sign), enabling him to create a solid customer network.

Due to the mutable Eight of Cups, much travel may be involved. The Knight is of the unpredictable air element, and he is placed beneath the earthy Devil, so questions arise: Are the people who are encouraging Bob going to support his enterprise with actual sales (Devil) when the time comes? Is Bob likely to engage in shady practices in order to obtain his goals? The proximity of the Eight of Cups also provokes questions: Is Bob's community ready to support his specific business? Has it been tried before and failed? Has he any hard research data to support his contention that his product is needed and timely, or are his aspirations built on an obsession and a dream?

The fifth card is the High Priestess, attributed to the Moon, so one of the powerful planetary trumps. With the first and second cards (both cardinal), the High Priestess emphasizes Bob's emotional investment in his new enterprise and his headlong rush in starting it. With the mutable Eight of Cups, it shows that Bob needs to take a break, get a fresh perspective, and evolve his business idea so that it more nearly matches the needs and mood of the community. He also should reconnect with old friends to gain an expanded base of support, as well as honest, unbiased opinions.

On a broader level, the High Priestess suggests accessing a counselor with wisdom about current business cycles and economic trends (Devil) that will influence his ultimate success, as the Moon rules all forms of cycles and the public. The Moon has a detrimental relationship with Capricorn (Devil), so her scope for comfortable flow and emotion is severely restrained by external or societal factors. On a personal level, Bob's inner emotions, comfort levels, and well-being (all Moon issues) are entwined with his enterprise to a dangerous degree (Devil). As an Aquarius, however, he may be choosing to ignore that facet of the situation, although it will cause him problems down the road.

Overall, the High Priestess placed over the Devil and the Knight of Swords suggests that Bob is jumping the gun with his idea. His idea is ahead of its time because of societal limitations and probably needs to be modified, transmuted, or postponed (Eight of Cups) until the community is ready to support his idea or until he can overcome restrictions (Devil).

Bearing in mind that Bob is obsessed and the reading is taking place in October (with the Sun currently transiting Libra), the zodiacal attributions give a good clue to timing. The first four cards in the spread supply all of the signs from Capricorn through Aries. This is the winter segment of the zodiac, the Sun signs from December through April. Bob needs to spend the next six months (fall until spring) rethinking his idea, networking, securing the support of other businesses, and ensuring his own mastery of the financial, legal, and tax aspects of his business. The Three of Wands and the Knight both suggest additional travels to observe the same type of business operating in another community (High Priestess—a mirror reflection, as the Moon reflects the Sun's light).

On a more personal level, Bob should also reassess how his business venture may erode his family life and friendships. The Eight of Cups and High Priestess indicate people in his life who may be jealous of the time he devotes to his self-chosen mission (Knight/Devil). His emotional boundaries (Devil) are inappropriate and will have an adverse impact on his loved ones (High Priestess/Moon in detriment with the Devil below her).

In this example, the High Priestess is free to interact with the other four cards without being tied to any particular sign, element, or mode—she isn't limited to a single dignity or influence. She's an independent agent who reacts and, in the Moon's case, reflects qualities of the other cards. As the card in the future position, there is an additional emphasis on time cycles as a crucial factor to Bob's plans. The Moon's phases in the coming months outline the timing for Bob: troubles or worries and restrained activity at the end of the year (when the Moon is new in Capricorn, her sign of detriment), with the potential for increasing success in the spring (when the Moon is new in Taurus, her sign of exaltation, and a fixed sign as suggested by the Knight of Swords).

## Example 2

Another client, Jane, is going on vacation, and she wants to know if her plans will go smoothly. A simple three-card spread, shown in figure 4, is used for this question.

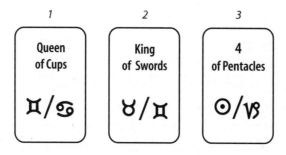

*Figure 4: Jane's Reading*

On the first scan, there doesn't appear to be any of the traditional "travel" cards in this spread. The first card is the Queen of Cups (21° Gemini to 20° Cancer). This card shows that Jane's travel plans involve her family (Cups/water) and that she is the one primarily responsible for initiating the trip and organizing the itinerary (cardinal). The Gemini part of this Queen is curious, so Jane has chosen to visit a place where she's never been before, probably a location near an ocean or lake (cardinal = new experiences).

The second card, King of Swords, emphasizes the mutable quality of Gemini (21° Taurus to 20° Gemini). The first thing that comes to mind here is a good map, which Jane has already studied. As this mutable sign rules communications and travel, Jane needs to double-check her flight and hotel reservations before leaving. Further, Jane's husband is looking forward to getting out of town, but isn't too thrilled about going to all of the places she's indicated or experimenting with varied cuisine at this vacation spot (the Taurus component of the King, fixed = conservative). This King and Queen share a mutable Gemini component, suggesting that both enjoy traveling. However, Jane's idea of spending a day visiting fashion warehouses (Cancer) does not appeal to the hubby, who would much rather be out on a golf course (Taurus), or the kids, who would prefer to watch TV and play in the ocean or swimming pool (Cancer).

The double accent on mutable Gemini is the clue here—Jane needs to be flexible and accommodate to everyone's tastes, and needs to solicit opinions from all of her family members as to their preferred activities.

The final card is the Four of Pentacles (Sun/Capricorn), a cardinal card. This clearly shows the hotel (Capricorn = buildings for collective use) as the stable base of operations for the family group while on vacation. It's near the beach, has a pool, and is within walking distance of a golf course. Jane can catch a bus (Capricorn = public services) to visit the fashion warehouses when she has time to be alone (cardinal = self-willed and directed), which leaves the rented car available for hubby and kids. They can organize a few days for family expeditions to see historic sites (Sun/Capricorn = organization, historic tradition), and come to a reasonable agreement about the types of restaurants they will visit, too (Taurus and Capricorn, both earthy and relate to food).

This final card shows how important it is to respect (cardinal sign Capricorn) each family member's individual preferences (Sun), while remaining organized, centralized, and in good communications with each other. Two cardinal cards bookend a central mutable card, showing the need for structured plans with room for flexibility.

### Example 3

Kim is a young woman trying to decide whether to accept a job offer. She's a Sun-sign Virgo (mutable earth) and also happens to know she has a Sagittarius Moon (mutable fire). She shuffles the deck and the three cards off the top are shown in figure 5.

Kim obviously has a dilemma. The Wheel (Jupiter) shows she's at a point of dramatic life changes. This is a planetary trump and very powerful in its influence over the following cards.

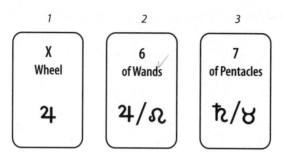

*Figure 5: Kim's Reading*

Luck seems to be on her side with the Six of Wands, a fixed-fire card; this indicates an interest in team activities, sports, and travel; it also shows she needs to use her energies creatively and in an environment with enough elbow room to be herself.

The dignity between the Wheel and the Six of Wands is very good. The Leo (fixed fire) component of the center card gives the planetary trump the capacity for steady development, personal courage in the face of change, and an optimistic outlook. Because Leo rules children, I ask Kim if she might already have an offer to work with kids somewhere, perhaps as a camp counselor.

She tells me that she does have an offer to work with kids this summer and she wants to accept it. This satisfies her Sagittarius Moon, which is playful, enjoys games and fun, and likes to travel.

The third card, the Seven of Pentacles, is the glitch! It is fixed earth, and it brings somber realities to bear upon this offer. The first and most obvious problem is scanty compensation; the second is location (earthy issues). Kim tells me that she wants to continue work on her elementary education degree, but the low pay and the extended work commitment out of town would compel her either to skip fall semester and get a second job, or to leave the job several weeks early in order to start the semester and get a part-time job to supplement her summer earnings. This card often expresses frustrating delays. Taurus, a fixed sign, emphasizes patience; and the number seven suggests that current issues have complex and contrary details attached to them.

This final card shows obstacles to her opportunity that won't go away and can't be ignored (fixed). Since she's a Sun-sign Virgo, the college plans are her top priority, but her Sagittarius Moon wants to go have a fun summer with the kids. It seems as though the most practical option is to find a better-paying job close to home for the summer.

But is that the end of the story? Heck, no! The Wheel is a tremendously powerful card, exerting influence on both the Six of Wands and the Seven of Pentacles. The Six of Wands is attributed to Jupiter/Leo, the Seven of Pentacles to Saturn/Taurus. This combination—double Jupiter, double fixed, plus Saturn, suggests that a wider, more collective evaluation of Kim's choices is appropriate.

I ask Kim if she is totally committed to a degree in elementary education and what her prospects for employment look like after she graduates (a Jupiter/Saturn issue). She says she had a hard time choosing a major, which is no big surprise since her mutable natal Sun and Moon signs are at odds. Further, her hometown has a declining population due to major layoffs (again, Jupiter/Saturn issue), so the school systems in the area are likely to be downsizing (Seven of Pentacles). Inevitably, she would have to relocate to another area to get a job.

The Wheel is starting to spin now! Because of her Virgo Sun, I ask Kim if she had considered any branches of medicine, particularly physical therapy (Seven of Pentacles). Yes, in fact, she had. And this field of study is available at her local college, with a thriving medical community that has plans to build a major addition to the hospital in the next few years.

What happened here? Originally the reading targeted a current job offer, but evolved into a discussion of her career plans. The two pip cards are both fixed, indicating a need to examine long-term plans and the dedication of time and resources necessary to gain results. The Wheel (Jupiter) is drawn into a fixed situation and is compelled to seek long-term growth through the resources at hand, both in educational prospects and in her hometown, where she would like to remain after graduation. The final combination of Jupiter (Six of Wands) and Saturn (Seven of Pentacles), the planets that define the relationship between the individual and the group, indicate that the parameters of Kim's summer job decision rest on a much broader foundation than just enjoyment or money. It's clear that she's aware of community changes that impact her future opportunities and limitations.

The Wheel as the first card shows that Kim is at an important crossroad of life: Should she choose a career that fulfills her love of education and children (her Sagittarius Moon), or should her choices serve her analytical and precision-oriented Virgo Sun? The chance job offer (Jupiter) is compelling her to view her career options realistically and may indicate a change of her major in college rather than accepting a job offer that delays her schooling and presents frustrating financial limitations. Ultimately, Kim has to make these decisions herself, but the question of a job offer was, in fact, only a corollary to the larger question of her initial career path after college graduation.

# CHAPTER 5

# NUMERIC DIGNITIES

**N**umeric dignities are a type of dignity specific to the tarot, card games, and cartomancy (divining with playing cards). Sets and sequences are a fundamental method of interpretation in cartomancy.[3] Nigel Jackson includes a short outline of the meaning of sets in the book that is included along with his deck.[4] The rules for several popular games base scoring on the acquisition of sets and sequences (poker, rummy, mah-jongg), and the tarot's history includes usage for play in a game called *tarrochi*, somewhat similar to bridge and euchre, where tricks are gained with the high card. It's appropriate, therefore, to include a discussion of these numeric forms of dignity as they apply to the tarot.

Sets occur when two or more cards of a numeric designation appear in a spread. A set of five occurs when the four pip cards of a digital denomination (for instance, the four Fours) include the trump card of the same number (the Emperor[5]). Although the impact of a set may be determined through the rules of cartomancy, the application of numerological meanings is also quite valid and may be more appropriate for the more mystically inclined tarot pack.[6]

---

3 See Marthy Jones, *It's in the Cards* (York Beach, Maine: Weiser, 1984).

4 See *The Nigel Jackson Tarot* (St. Paul, Minn.: Llewellyn, 2000).

5 Some tarot decks have alternative numbering given for the trumps (the Major Arcana); the numbering here given is found in many modern decks, although there are certainly exceptions to this pattern. Some decks omit numbering in the trumps altogether—the choice of numbering system is at the discretion of the reader.

6 Readers seeking deeper knowledge of numerology and tarot are encouraged to read Faith Javane and Dusty Bunker, *Numerology and the Divine Triangle* (Atglen, Pa.: Whitford Press, 1979), which provides the meanings of numbers with the related tarot cards, as well as various techniques of numerology.

# THE MEANINGS OF SETS
# AS INTERPRETED NUMEROLOGICALLY

The numerologically derived meanings of sets are merely a starting point, as sets are also influenced by the cards included by element and mode, as well as by their placement in a neighborhood. Sets are not restricted to cards drawn sequentially in the layout but may be analyzed as an emphasized numeric vibration regardless of where they appear in a spread. It should be noted that a set is more powerful when the matching cards appear in a contiguous formation in the spread—in a horizontal or vertical line, or in a diagonal line (see Demonstration 2 in chapter 12). Nevertheless, the appearance of two or more of a kind, even if scattered throughout the zones of a layout, places special emphasis on the numeric vibration of the set. For instance, if a pair of Sixes appear in a five-card spread, the numeric vibration of the number 6 suggests that the querent has life situations that are reaching a perfect stage of development. Perfection is impossible to retain for any length of time, so further development is inevitable. A 6 doesn't last very long!

Single-digit trump cards are directly related to similarly numbered pips. Trump cards numbered above ten also have a numeric relationship to pip cards by reducing the double to a single digit. For example, the Hanged Man, as the twelfth trump, can have a numeric relation to the number 3 by adding the digits of twelve together: $1 + 2 = 3$. If this method of reduction is used, there may be—theoretically—the possibility of six or seven of a kind in a spread. Let's look at each of the numbered cards in turn.

## Ace

The number 1 is a seed, and these seeds are characteristic of the element of their suit. The appearance of multiple Aces in a spread is quite fortunate; the querent should expect element-related beginnings in his or her life.

**Pair:** Two separate beginnings for the querent (according to Lady Circe, the high priestess of the Toledo Wiccan community, the Ace of

Swords and the Ace of Cups together means "a change of place and a change of pace").

**Three:** Good luck, news of birth and marriage.

**Four:** Supreme blessings, triumph.

**Five:** (four Aces + Magician or Wheel or Sun): Magic, the manifestation of wishes and desires through pure intention. The four elements and spirit united in purpose.

## Two

The number 2 is the singularity of the 1 reflecting upon the other. This number implies opposition, duality, division, flux, and change.

**Pair:** Ebb and flow, cyclic issues require further thought.

**Three:** Exchanges, transactions, development of ideas.

**Four:** Turning points in diverse situations; the querent is bombarded with change.

**Five:** (four Twos + High Priestess, Justice, or Judgment): Life in a state of total flux and change; parallel evolution is intertwined between querent and situations in the environment.

## Three

The number 3 is the number of fertility and creativity. The Greeks knew this number as "the first perfection,"[7] as 3 shows the result of the joining of the 1 and the 2.

**Pair:** Focus on work, productivity.

---

7 Dr. John Opsopaus, from a lecture given at the World Tarot Congress, May 2002.

**Three:** Making progress in goals; choices are necessary for further development.

**Four:** Accomplishment, recognition, and reward for efforts.

**Five:** (four Threes + Empress, Hanged Man, or the World): Abundant fertility, joy in work, notable progress.

## Four

The number 4 is the number of foundation. There are four elements, and in this number, a stage of initial stability is taking place. A square has four corners, and this is a very stable and well-grounded geometric shape. The productive capacity of the 3 has come to a point of rest, where the identity is solidified.

**Pair:** Promises are kept, invitations to events.

**Three:** Agreements, contracts, unity of purpose.

**Four:** Long-lasting results, immortal quality.

**Five:** (four Fours + Emperor or Death): Formal agreements that are the foundation of long-lasting structures in historic events.

## Five

The number 5 brings chaos to the placid 4. A new condition disrupts the stability and identity founded in the 4, so this number tends to be unsettling unless it's the querent who is adding the new condition. The number 5 implies a level of unpredictability from a group dynamic, as emotions and the intellect churn at cross-purposes.

**Pair:** Turmoil, outer forces at work, unexpected changes come due to others.

**Three:** Accidents, losses.

**Four:** Chaos, ill-luck, disintegration of set purposes and goals.

**Five:** (four Fives + Hierophant or Temperance): Chaos with spiritual factors; blind fate fulfills a higher purpose unseen by the querent.

## Six

The number 6 restores equilibrium and continuity from the disruption of the 5. This number is the "second perfection" and brings welcome evolution of the particular element to its most beautiful form. Sixes are lucky cards. As mentioned above, though, this state of perfection is rarely of extended endurance.

**Pair:** Benefits come through others; favors.

**Three:** Good travels, luck comes through friends and associates.

**Four:** Great success in ambitions, public acclaim.

**Five:** (four Sixes + Lovers or Devil): Luck in love and money; great happiness.

## Seven

The number 7 is mystic and deep. The beauty of the number 6 is beginning to erode. The spiritual quality and character of each element is being tested at this point in the numeric sequence. A preponderance of the number 7 in a reading should always be seen as a mandate for the querent to reach for spiritual and philosophical solutions, and above all, to be patient in the process that he or she is experiencing.

**Pair:** Delays; decisions should not be rushed.

**Three:** Frustration in different areas; conflict of interest.

**Four:** Prayerful waiting and tests of character; long-term issues are at stake.

**Five:** (four Sevens + Chariot or Tower): The inner control of the querent is being tested in a fateful manner. Many factors are up in the air, awaiting resolution, yet the querent must remain centered and grounded regardless of provocation and inner doubts.

## Eight

The number 8 suggests the need to make choices and work diligently to overcome the uncertainty of the 7. The querent's judgment and dedication are being tested. Trust in self and others is also put to the test. Where the Eight of Wands and Pentacles are both cards of a positive nature, the Eight of Swords and Cups are both rather forlorn. The consistency of the set has great bearing on the interpretation, so the meanings given below are merely an outline that will be further defined by the specific participants.

**Pair:** Attention to detail, timing is critical.

**Three:** Tests of intellectual analysis, ability to fruitfully critique conditions at hand before choices are made.

**Four:** Solemn judgments about the life path.

**Five:** (four Eights + Strength or the Star): With Strength, this set demands an analysis of the the querent's core identity and roles through an assessment of the skills and resources at hand. With the Star card, this set tests the querent's ability to apply judgments to the process of life-structuring, relevant to both interpersonal relationships and visions of future goals. Obtrusive or unrealistic concepts need to be eliminated at this stage, requiring ruthless honesty and enormous strength of will to carry through with decisions.

## Nine

The number 9 signals the end of the single-digit numeric sequence. It contains all that went before and represents the final results of the development of each element in the suits. This is the "third perfection," the numeric stage of manifestation that precedes the death of the element in the 10. As such, the number 9 is highly significant because it reveals how the choices of the querent that were necessitated by interaction (the 5s) are now results (9s) determined by the querent's previous choices. Once more, the Nines in the tarot are split between two positive (Nine of Pentacles and Cups), one neutral (Nine of Wands) and one negative (Nine of Swords). Delineation should be fine-tuned by suit.

**Pair:** Questions from the past influence the present situation.

**Three:** Watchfulness and caution are advisable.

**Four:** Surrounded by friends or adversaries.

**Five:** (four Nines + Hermit or the Moon): Action is dependent upon wisdom; no errors can be made without unwanted consequences. The querent must acknowledge how his or her prior decisions have led to this point and must find the courage and strategies to proceed in the situation.

## Ten

The number 10 is the final in the sequence. The incontrovertible evidence of the development of the element is seen here. The 10 represents endings, conclusions, and finalities. This number also bears the influence of the group upon the individual. Since the 1 is combined with a 0, each ending contains the potential seed for a new beginning, found in the Ace. The relationship between Tens and Aces is a close one and to some extent may be considered as a kind of evolving set within a reading where they are combined. The Magician and the Wheel are similarly related through this numeric dignity between 1s and 10s.

**Pair:** Lasting gains or losses.

**Three:** Conclusions regarding people and property.

**Four:** Total collapse of current life path, leading to rebirth in a new form.

**Five:** (four Tens + Wheel or Sun): Endings that are tied to the direction the querent is moving on the Wheel of Life. Positions in the spread will indicate whether this is leading up or down. Meaningful purpose is implied by this combination, although it may not be immediately evident.

## Beyond Numerology

Sets are sensitive to location and suit composition, and they are further defined by the elemental and modal qualities of their neighbors. A set that is smaller than five of a kind that contains the numerically related trump card will partake of the more esoteric qualities of the number. Readers may find that other delineations of the sets such as the study of numbers as they are related to the sephiroth in the Kabbala are pertinent and may wish to add notes to the above listings.

The observation of the overall numeric content of a spread provides information regarding the level of change and dynamics in the querent's life. Lower numbers are initiatory and preparatory, whereas the higher numbers, particularly Nines and Tens, will indicate a greater propensity for dramatic transition.

## SEQUENCES

Sequences occur within the numeric content of the tarot pack and are naturally contained in the pip cards of each suit, Ace through Ten, and within the trumps, numbered 0 to XXI. Rising numbers imply growth, development, and evolution, while decreasing numbers imply deterioration, diminishment, or regression. This simple concept always works when viewing a sequence in a spread.

Many forms of sequences may be seen in a layout. A sequence does not need to contain cards of only one suit; however, a one-suit sequence is more notable. Sequences also occur in the court cards, as status rises from the Princess to the King, and may rise from pips to court cards (Nine, Ten, Princess). A trump sequence is quite powerful, and the numeric segment displayed by a trump sequence should be interpreted as a thematic element in the reading.

Sequences of pip cards should also be considered for their modal content. For instance, a sequence of Seven, Eight, Nine moves from fixed to mutable (i.e., from rigid to bendable). While the lower digits are more dynamic (Two, Three, Four are cardinal), the higher digits (Eight, Nine, Ten) are more spiritual and influenced by the collective situation shown in a spread. A sequence of the central digits (Five, Six, Seven) is the most difficult because of its fixed nature. Where the cardinal pips show a process that is beginning, if the process is seen from the outset as having faulty properties, it can be halted before it goes too far. A mutable sequence is the end of the process and must be accepted as evidence of what was put into the process at its initiation. A fixed sequence is unavoidable and must be faced squarely, whether rising or falling. Matters have gone too far to stop, yet are not far enough to simply accept as a consequence or outcome.

One of the most powerful sequences occurs when there is a "straight flush," a numeric sequence of cards from the same suit. This type of sequence shows the phase of development as an underlying process for neighboring cards. A "royal flush," with all court cards, is quite dynamic and increases the power of the element shown by the suit. A more subtle form of sequence occurs when a court card is matched by cards of its zodiacal property, for instance, if the Queen of Pentacles is joined by the Two and Three of Pentacles (all Capricorn).

A sequence of two or more suits blurs the force of the elements and relies more firmly on the sector of numeric sequence that appears. Instead of the elements affecting the progression of the numbers, the numbers affect the development of the elements. An example of a two-suit sequence is shown in figure 6 on page 56: Six of Pentacles, Seven of Swords, Eight of Pentacles.

Numerically, the perfection of the Six moves to the tests of the Seven, and results are found in the Eight. Elementally, the pair of Pentacles suggests the development of a material product. The beautiful gift offered in the Six of Pentacles is subjected to scrutiny of purpose in the Seven of Swords. Some issues of applicability or broad outreach may prove the item less than suitable for distribution on a large scale. The value of pure beauty is subjected to fickle public opinion. The Eight of Pentacles as the final card of the sequence

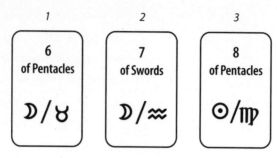

Figure 6: A Two-Suit Sequence

suggests that the product is being refined for more general purposes. While the dominant idea (Pentacles) remains, the product moves from beauty to utility as intellectual scrutiny (Swords) results in distinct choices about the item.

Sequences of three suits (or possibly four) are even more reliant on the numeric content. Yet the elements of the suits involved should be considered in order to form a more accurate delineation of the sequence. The modal content is also more critical. For example, consider the three-suit sequence shown in figure 7: Seven of Wands, Eight of Swords, Nine of Cups.

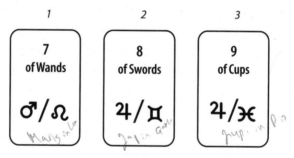

Figure 7: A Three-Suit Sequence

In this sequence, the tests of the Seven move to the decisive choices of the Eight and produce the results of refinement (or degradation) found in the Nine. The Seven is fixed, and the Eight and Nine are mutable. The elemental series is: fire, air, water. A possible delineation of this sequence is: the fiery focus of effort is embattled by challenges, a situation that results in an airy suspension, intellectual gridlock that halts process. Once joined by the watery element, the source of illumination (the fiery Seven) that was blocked by intellectual scrutiny and anxiety (the airy Eight) regains its free flow, restored through the property of love. The astrological attributions of these cards provide further depth to the interpretation: Mars/Leo (Seven), Jupiter/Gemini (Eight), Jupiter/Pisces (Nine). Fiery Leo is required to demonstrate a show of force (Mars); airy Gemini is perplexed and stymied by excessive (Jupiter) development of thought; both finally require the loving, spiritual, and compassionate qualities of Jupiter in Pisces (rulership for this planet) in order to succeed. In the simplest terms, in this case, the Father (fire) and the Son (air) can't succeed without the qualities of the Mother (water).

## INTERRELATIONSHIPS IN SETS AND SEQUENCES

Sets and sequences in a spread outline the thrust of the storyline of the querent's situation. Court cards in the neighborhood of a sequence show who is closely involved with the process, and the comparison of the elements of the court cards and the set or sequence will show whether this involvement has a positive or negative effect. For example, if the fixed-mode sequence Five, Six, and Seven of Pentacles appears in a spread, and the Knight of Swords is placed nearby, the Knight's intellectual prowess is undermining development of the earthy product. Indeed, he may be the devil's advocate, questioning every point of the process. His role in the situation may be irritating, but necessary (fixed). Another example: the Four, Five and Six of Cups with the King of Pentacles. Increasing attachment and affection are indicated by the pip sequence, but the process is slowed by the earthy King as he subjects the flowing water to practical considerations like trustworthiness, ease of application, and appropriateness. While the King may not be halting this process, the role he plays in slowing the sequence may not be pleasing to the querent.

Sequences of court cards show the quality of interrelationship in the querent's various environments. Generally, Wands/Swords and Cups/Pentacles form the most favorable partnerships, and this will remain the case unless the court cards are separated by a difficult pip or trump card. If neutral or hostile elemental court-card combinations appear, the surrounding cards will determine the origin and nature of their attitudes. Pips determine the quality of their exchange by element and mode. Even a same-suit couple can suffer from the presence of a hostile-suit pip card, but the nature of the suffering may be temporary, or may be averted through unity of purpose to overcome the problem. Figure 8 shows the King of Cups, Nine of Swords, and Queen of Cups. The royal couple is separated by the unhappy Nine of Swords (Mars/Gemini, airy, mutable, refinement/degradation of the element).

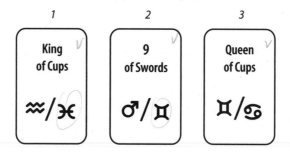

*Figure 8: A Hostile Pip*

Although this couple shares the natural affinity of suit, the Nine of Swords shows that they are separated by hostilities and resentments, by distance, fears, or conflicts of interest. Since the Queen of Cups is attributed to the Gemini-Cancer cusp, the Nine of Swords relates more to the Queen than to the King. It can be inferred that she may be the source of the separation or has some ideas that reflect badly upon the King and are the source of the division between them. Another possible interpretation suggested by this trio of cards is that a marriage (Queen) is being disputed by relatives who disapprove of the union (Nine of Swords and King). Both the King and the Nine of Swords are mutable and relate to group signs, Gemini and Pisces. Once again, the initiative of marriage between two individuals (the cardinal Queen) is the source of the tensions displayed in the Nine of Swords.

Further interpretation of this trio would be reliant upon surrounding cards, but this brief example, I hope, conveys some idea of how the pip and court cards can interact through mode, element, and sequence. The same technique may be applied to a set of court cards (that is, two knights, three princesses, etc.). The dignity of the court and pip cards should be determined by element, mode, and attribution to determine the most accurate assessment of their interrelated influence. The court card that is most closely related by dignity to a neighboring pip card usually has the most to do with the pip card's implications.

Sets and sequences of court cards that are neighbored by trump cards should be regarded very differently. Trump cards suggest pervasive influence of formative energies. The individuals suggested by the court cards will experience the specific influence of the trump card more or less equally, unless they share the trump card's attribution. A court card that is related to a trump card will experience the influence of the trump most keenly, as the individual represented by that court card may be the reason the trump is appearing in the spread. This is an issue of the interconnectedness of individuals and inevitably occurs when people who are closely associated share the experience of triumph or crisis. In figure 9—King of Swords, Queen of Pentacles, Devil—the Queen of Pentacles is attributed to the Sagittarius/Capricorn cusp, so she shares an attribution with the Devil (Capricorn). Therefore, she more keenly experiences the difficulties of the Devil card, both by neighboring placement and attribution.

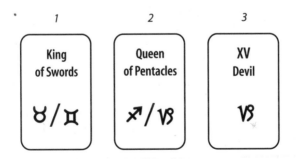

*Figure 9: Trump Card with Court Cards*

But the King of Swords is caught up in the Queen's problems and may be acting as an advisor, lawyer, or consultant as she faces her issues. He may also be able to help her see her devilish situation in a more detached manner through his intellectual viewpoint. Although his airy element is neutral to her earthy element, it is probably just what the Queen needs in dealing with the Devil. His capacity for dispassionate assessment can help her avoid falling into a state of morose introspection.

•  •  •

Although the root of sets and sequences can be found in card games and cartomancy, their application in the tarot is undeniably important. Elemental dignity and modal dignity are tools necessary to assessing the impact of sets and sequences in a tarot layout. These will be most obvious in a smaller spread (three to five cards), and the relationships more closely entwined. However, with careful scrutiny, sets and sequences can be identified in larger spreads. Even when the cards of a set or sequence are not contiguous (i.e., immediate neighbors), the relationship is still inferred when the conditions of a set or sequence are met within the group of cards that appear in a spread. A contiguous set/sequence is obviously more dominant in meaning and impact, whereas a more scattered set/sequence has a more diluted or subtle impact on the entire delineation.

# CHAPTER 6

# PLANETARY TRUMPS AS FREE AGENTS

T o review material from previous chapters, the twenty-two Major Arcana (trump cards) are assigned to three categories of attributions: zodiacal, elemental, and planetary. The zodiacal trumps have both elemental and modal dignity. The elemental trumps provide an essence-related dignity for surrounding cards. Elemental trumps embody the ancient concept of pure substances that underlie all forms of existence in the universe. The elemental trumps personify the impact of elements in their purest forms, transcending modes, signs, and numeric significance until juxtaposed next to other cards that supply those qualities.

Planetary trumps function a bit differently. Planets are neighbors of Earth circling the Sun, the bright star at the center of our system. They visibly move through the constellations (which are fixed, or unmoving) when above the horizon and may disappear for several months when below the horizon or when too close to the Sun from our viewpoint on Earth. The word *planets* is derived from the Greek *planetoi,* which means "travelers," and these travelers are named for gods in the Greco-Roman pantheon. These gods have specific character traits and are the protagonists in mythic legends. The gods are free agents, imbued with immortal powers and capacities that transcend human abilities. The planetary gods are unencumbered by human morality, so they are at liberty to indulge in acts both benefic and amoral.

By contrast, the signs of the zodiac are constellations composed of stars that appear seasonally, due to Earth's orbit around the Sun. There are hundreds of constellations, and the twelve chosen to represent the zodiac merely have the virtue of appearing along the ecliptic.[8] These groups of stars are at an enormous distance from our solar system. The trump cards attributed to signs of the zodiac provide environmental settings that relate to the things, specialties, traits, and qualities of each sign. The planetary trumps relate and respond to these settings, as they color the behavior (sign), energy levels (mode), and object identification (element) of the attributed planet through dignity relationships.

Planets do have affinities to signs and elements, and they give their most characteristic performances in their signs of preference. This is the basis for the astrological concept of dignity. Planets have designated zodiacal signs of ruler-ship, exaltation, fall, and detriment. They also experience dignity or debility by virtue of being positioned within the twelve houses of a horoscope. This is dig-nity conferred by location, astrologically termed *accidental dignity.* The term for the tarot equivalent of this concept, more thoroughly discussed in chapter 10, is *locational dignity.* An example of locational dignity: the Emperor will func-tion at his best as the first card drawn (Aries is the first sign) or at the top of a spread (or in a worldly position). The Emperor would be debilitated at the bottom of a spread (or in a domestic position), where he'll be stuck in the kitchen washing dishes, unable to exert much of his masterful influence on events.

In some systems of elemental dignity, the planetary trumps are assigned elements, thereby committing each planet to the element of a sign they rule. This is problematic because, of the seven traditional planets, all but the Sun and Moon rule two signs of differing elements. This system implies that the signs "own" their ruling planets. Secondly, it limits the planets to a single elemental type of expression. Planets are always in motion and travel through all of the signs of the zodiac at varying speeds. A transiting[9] planet reveals a unique facet of its personality in each sign.

Emancipated from the conceptual straitjacket of elemental association, the planetary trumps are free to exert a far-ranging, independent influence

---

8 The ecliptic is the Via Solis, the path that the Sun and the planets appear to take around the Earth. It is the *geocentric,* or earth-centered, viewpoint.
9 "Transiting" means to travel through a sign.

on neighboring cards. Planet-attributed trumps partake of the mythically assigned traits of each planet. These traits are enacted through their proximity to cards in a spread, the ease, discomfort, or likely behavior of which is determined by their dignity with nearby cards. Neighboring cards show topical content and environmental factors that qualify these planetary players: their motivations and energy flow. The zone may either be favorable or display critical stumbling blocks to their effectiveness. Planetary trumps course outward to encounter other cards and are fully embodied by the details of the spread's zone (see chapter 12: Demonstration 1, the Empress card).

## PLANETARY TRUMP CARDS

### Moon

The Moon is attributed to the High Priestess. This "light"[10] orbits Earth every twenty-eight days, passing through a zodiac sign (thirty degrees of arc) in about two and a half days, roughly twelve degrees of arc per day. While the Moon vastly prefers Cancer (her watery sign of rulership) and Taurus (her earthy sign of exaltation), she exhibits strengths and weaknesses in the other ten signs that contribute a more comprehensive understanding of the Moon in all of her phases.

The Moon has approximately thirteen new and full cycles each year. Every month, she is new in the sign where the Sun is transiting (for instance, a New Moon in late July is in Leo, as the Moon joins the Sun in this sign) and is full every month in the sign opposite of the Sun (a Full Moon in early May is full in Scorpio, opposite of the Sun in Taurus). Since the Moon is both new and full in every zodiac sign each year and will pass through every zodiac sign at least thirteen times a year, it's hardly fair to limit her to a single element. In fact, no other planet embodies the sheer range of zodiacal expression as distinctly as the Moon.

---

10 The Sun and Moon are more properly referred to as "lights," but may be called planets to simplify expression.

As a planetary goddess, the Moon rules cycles and phases. She rules the unconscious mind, dreams, the bond between mother and infant, the breasts and their nurturing milk, and the cycles of feminine fertility—menarche, menstruation, and menopause. (In fact, if a woman draws the High Priestess as the first card in a reading, she may be on her period!) The Moon represents the full range of human emotion and feeling, from the ecstatic to the despairing. She is secretive and mysterious in her capacity as the High Priestess, and she possesses the wisdom of time, eternal memory, and potential for fertility.

As ruler of the unconscious, the Moon has dominion over the inaccessible and uncharted depths of the mind. This is an important facet of the High Priestess, for she has mastered the difficult journey that the conscious mind must take in passing through the "veil" to access these hidden realms. This realm is irrational and does not operate by an identifiable set of rules; nor can it be reached through mechanical or rational means. The Moon is a companion to Earth and, in many mythologies, a consort to the Sun.

Her dark side represents loneliness, isolation, and sorrow. Her bright side is a reflection of the Sun's light, indicating the blending of emotions that encourage interdependency. The Moon is like a movie screen, so it encompasses the Jungian concept of the "projection" of an animus or anima image that one person may unconsciously place on another.

The High Priestess's most compatible trump cards are the Hierophant (Taurus) and the Chariot (Cancer). In the Hierophant, we see how her cyclic phases of light are dependent on the Sun, while her orbit's center of gravity is Earth. The Moon is our most visible example of how cycles of time and destiny that are experienced by humanity are a corollary to the cycles of the universe. The Hierophant understands the cycles of time and space, and the High Priestess is his interpreter and a channel into the underlying awareness of the human organism. The High Priestess emphasizes the tides of life with the Chariot—how human lives ebb and flow, develop, evolve, and wane in the pattern of growth cycles.

The High Priestess struggles greatly with the Devil, as the Moon is in detriment in Capricorn. This is the sign of authority and limitation ruled by Saturn, the Lord of Karma. Karma is the work and learning process that all incarnate forms must endure. The Devil is the reality of temptations and lusts and their overwhelming lures to the senses and sensual desires, no matter how badly these may damage the individual who cedes control to them. These qualities are offensive to the solemn and pervasive inner eye of the Priestess, who desires belonging and unity through transcending the confines of ego and material attachment.

The Queen of Cups (Cancer) and the Knight of Pentacles (Taurus) enact some of the Moon's most basic planetary characteristics, and they serve her purposes. In the pip cards, the High Priestess will express in true form near the Two, Three, and Four of Cups and the Five, Six, and Seven of Pentacles. Her capacity for darker emotions will be triggered near cards attributed to Mars and Saturn or Capricorn and Scorpio. A preferred location for the High Priestess is at the bottom of a spread, or in a spread position or sector connected with emotional or familial concerns.

## Venus

The planet Venus is attributed to the Empress. This planet orbits the Sun in 288 days and always appears to be close to the Sun because her orbit is inside Earth's. Venus and Mars have complex orbital patterns that symbolically enact the story of Mars pursuing Venus. They are considered a *planetary pair.*

Venus has rulership over love and beauty and things that give or create pleasure, particularly sensual pleasure. In a psychological sense, Venus rules values: goals or things that each individual wishes to attain or obtain more than all others. In astrology, the values of Venus are personalized according to sign, house, and aspects with other planets. Similarly, in tarot these values can be identified by the Empress in proximity to other cards. Where she appears in a spread will give a good idea of what is desired. This card is associated with the arts, culture, harmony, and cooperation; dance, music, and rhythm; and valuable possessions such as jewelry. The goddess Venus always desires fine adornments, so clothing and cosmetics fall under her rule. She is fertile and desirable, fully a woman.

Venus—with all of her desires and pleasures—is not particularly moral. Her darker qualities include jealousy, envy, and covetousness, and she may ruthlessly employ her feminine wiles to obtain her ends regardless of the impact on others. She is also prone to rages and tempers if thwarted. She expects her lovers to be faithful to her and give her great adoration, but doesn't return the courtesy of fidelity to others. In some ways, she can be a petulant child, and her punishments for offense are cruel and heartless. This is a side of the Empress that will be observed if the card is reversed or in ill-dignity.

The cycles of Venus include a period of rising in the east in the morning (Venus Lucifer) and a period of rising in the west in the evening (Venus Hesperides). These orbital phases show two contrasting sides of this planet: the feisty, lusty, and jubilant morning personality, and her sophisticated and cultivated evening persona. These are akin to her behavior in her two signs of rulership. With the Hierophant (Taurus), she is more concerned with possessions, wealth, talent, security, and obtaining sources and outlets for passions. This is her earthy side of physical and material values. With Justice (Libra), her precocious desire for romantic relationships, harmony, and cooperation, as well as supreme taste in the arts, decor, and tranquil surroundings is emphasized. This is the airy side of artistic, communicative, and interpersonal values, desiring the perfection of order and balance. At all times, however, Venus is concerned with self-value, and she promotes a dominant image of desirability, capability, and talent.

The Empress card expresses these Venusian qualities. When well-dignified, she expresses love, beauty, physical pleasures, pregnancy, luxuries, and feminine adornment. In ill-dignity, she may embody the old adage: "Hell hath no fury like a woman scorned." Even Jupiter avoided her when she displayed her bitchy, grasping nature. The Empress will be most congenial with the Hierophant and Justice, and she may mitigate some of the more difficult divinatory meanings of the Moon card. She will be disturbed in close proximity to the Death card and may reveal her cruel, amoral nature near the Emperor unless accompanied by favorable neighbors. Her Minor Arcana (court and pip) cards of native comfort and affinity are the Knight of Pentacles; the Queen of Swords; the Five, Six, and Seven of Pentacles (Taurus); and the Two, Three, and Four of Swords (Libra). The Empress behaves most erratically near the Five, Six, and Seven of Cups (Scorpio), and she will experience the capacity for domination near the Two and Three of Wands because of their Aries attribution. Venus is attributed to the Four of Wands, so this card gives a most positive expression next to the Empress.

In locational dignity, the Empress will function best in relationship and partnership positions (the seventh house in a twelve-house spread), and in positions connected with money and gain (second house). She will also enjoy spread positions that regard love and sex. The Empress is a favorable card in most circumstances, but it's important to note if she is ill-dignified by neighbors or if any surrounding cards show that her desires may be thwarted.

## Mercury

Mercury is attributed to the Magician. This planet is extremely important in astrology, as it functions (much like the Moon) in a variety of subtle ways. Mercury is closest to the Sun, orbiting the star in only eighty-eight days. From Earth, Mercury always appears very close to the Sun, and it has about three retrogrades a year. Where the Moon rules cycles and the unconscious, Mercury represents the conscious mind and cycles of awareness and perception. Mercury rules a wide variety of things, because this is a god that got around a lot! Even as a day-old infant he was up to hijinks, but this greatly amused and pleased his father, Jupiter. Though born to the nymph Maia (thus only semidivine), Mercury finagled his way up to full divinity within a few days of his birth. Whenever this god is involved in a myth, it's never boring.

This planet contains a multitude of ever-changing faces and functions, which is why Mercury is so perfectly attributed to the Magician. At his lowest level, Mercury rules thieves and tricksters, jugglers and jesters, mountebanks and charlatans. Mercury is a practical joker and always capable of eluding retribution with alibis and excuses. Although he uses his silver tongue to wiggle out of punishments, this verbal ability relates to the more noble attributes of language, writing, poetry, and invention. Mercury designates skills and virtuosity and represents artists or craftspeople who have studied and practiced for so long that they seem to perform magic. In this aspect, his attributes include teaching and learning, the ability to perceive and understand, and the capacity for thinking and intuiting. It may seem odd that a single planet should encompass both logic and intuition, but there you have it.

Another role of Mercury is as god of the crossroads, and he gets his Greek name, Hermes, from the stones, herms, that were placed at the junctions of roadways. He rules commerce and trade, negotiations, bartering, and travel. As these are areas of life that tend to lead to expansion, this planet shows its capacity for carrying out the wishes of Jupiter. Mercury is Jupiter's errand boy, conveying messages from the heights of Olympus to the depths of Tartarus (the underworld). He is sent to guide mortals on their quests, and Hades gives him the caduceus as a symbol of his role in guiding the dead to the underworld. Because he was such a precocious youngster, Mercury is connected with child prodigies, siblings, and the activities of the young— and this is apt because humans begin to absorb a language and familial relationships at a very early age.

At its highest level, Mercury is the sorcerer, the magician, the alchemist. This can be seen in later legends of Mercury as the creator of the world, the creator of the Word. Leave it to Mercury to connive his way into the top position, right? The alchemical view of Mercury was as *Mercurius duplex, utriusque capax*, which translates as: Mercury, double and capable of either (or both), a sublime entity who is the transformer as well as the substance being transformed.[11] Mercury the Magus can subtly blend words, sounds, ideas, and ingredients. Here is the concept of Mercury as a shape-shifter, creator of illusion and magic of the highest sort. The metal quicksilver, or mercury, gives a good example of this elusive behavior. Its common use in thermometers demonstrates how Mercury can detect minute changes in the environment— an aspect of perception. This aspect of the Magician card is applicable when one is reading for doctors, psychologists, research scientists, and physicists (or other tarotists or astrologers).

This description of Mercury is far from complete but may give the reader an idea of the range of concepts and functions assigned to this planet. As the

---

11 Liz Greene and Howard Sasportas. *The Inner Planets: Building Blocks of Personal Reality* (York Beach, Maine: Weiser, 1993), pp. 22-23.

planet attributed to the Magician card, one may see how slippery he is, how indefinable and hard to pin down to a single, simple meaning. Therefore, this card is extremely sensitive to dignity and placement in a spread. Like the High Priestess and her light and dark phases, Mercury has a distinctly cyclic character, and if he feels that he lacks a mode of expression, he's capable of inventing one! For this reason, the Magician must be observed with exceptional perspicacity, with an eye to spotting clues in neighboring cards as to the possible avenue for his various characteristics. His comfortable trump friends are the Lovers (Gemini) and the Hermit (Virgo). His more troublesome side will manifest near the Moon (Pisces), as his mental capacities may be flooded with intense emotions, and his sharp mind overwhelmed. The Temperance card (Sagittarius) may provoke the Magician to overdo his act or overcompensate for missing qualities, or indeed through sheer exaggeration. With the right surroundings in a spread, this combination could be considered the Supreme B.S. Machine.

Since Mercury lies inside Earth's orbit, this planet has two important cycles in the sky: as Promethean Mercury, a morning star; and as Epimethean Mercury, an evening star. Promethean Mercury relates to Mercury in his rulership of Gemini (Lovers)—with brilliant, original thoughts, an interest in a wide range of topics, and with infinite modes of expression. Epimethean Mercury is more like Mercury in his rulership of Virgo (Hermit): careful, cautious, and conservative in thought; concerned with history, protocol, and precedent; detail-oriented and scholarly. This is the analytical Mercury, capable of the meticulous research and thorough observation necessary to comprehending a specific area of study.

Mercury retrogrades[12] in all twelve zodiac signs in a four- to five-year period. During these retrograde periods, Mercury is focused on the inner

---

12 Mercury retrogrades occur when Mercury passes in front of the Sun (called an Inferior Conjunction). In this position, a Mercury retrograde is physically much more like an eclipse or a New Moon. At the opposite side of this cycle, Mercury passes behind the Sun in direct motion (called a Superior Conjunction) and marks the transition from its morning to evening phase. Although astrologers continue to term this cycle as a "retrograde," the concept of an eclipse is more to the point. The retrograde cycles of Venus are similar—she passes in front of the Sun. Only planetary retrogrades that occur outside Earth's orbit are technically "retrogrades," where the planet appears to move backward in the sky.

workings of the mind, on the past, on self-discovery or rediscovery. Each year, this planet concentrates on a specific element for its three retrogrades and generally moves to another element in the following year. The Magician is particularly notable if it comes up in a spread during a Mercury retrograde cycle, as it may indicate specific issues that the querent must handle during that retrograde.

Because Mercury has so many areas of dominion, when the Magician card is in difficulty there can be great trouble with the senses, both the sources and organs of perception. Dyslexia, autism, blindness, deafness, or other handicaps may be indicated. Furthermore, there may be difficulties with mental or emotional problems like manic-depression, psychosis, or sociopathic tendencies. This is where the inner alchemy of human chemistry goes astray. Mercury is closely connected with criminals, particularly with thieves and burglars, but a particularly ill-dignified Magician must be watched for making other people disappear—by abduction or possible murder. Mercury is completely amoral—a fact one should never forget in connection with the Magician! His father, Jupiter, is the only god who can compel Mercury to make reparations after his thefts and tricks, so a strong paternal influence is essential in dealing with an ill-dignified Magician.

With the Minor Arcana cards, the Magician will prefer the King of Pentacles and the King of Swords; the Eight, Nine, and Ten of Swords and the Eight, Nine, and Ten of Pentacles all enhance his qualities of mutability, acquisitiveness, and shape shifting. Bearing in mind the general meanings of the last three Sword pip cards, this may not be to the advantage of the querent unless strongly indicated. The Magician will tend to be at odds with the Kings of Wands and Cups—they will be uncomfortable with his slippery ways and smooth talking. The same is true with the Eight, Nine, and Ten of Cups. Astrologically, Mercury is in detriment in Sagittarius, the ruling sign of the Eight, Nine, and Ten of Wands. When the Magician is next to these cards, he will have to work harder to express himself, to perform well without overkill.

In locational dignity, the Magician is quite fluid and handy to have around unless particularly ill-dignified. Mercury is a smooth operator and generally finds a way to get along wherever he may find himself. In the center of a reading, the Magician will indicate the thoughts and ideas of the querent, or particularly important messages or transactions. The Magician needs careful observation in relationship positions, as neighboring cards will show his reliability or lack thereof. At the top of a spread, the Magician will indicate a person with an impact on the outcomes of a situation. Because of his connection with intellectual matters, the Magician will have a bearing on the querent's career path or on professional people with whom the querent may be in contact. Take note if the Magician is joined with the High Priestess—this pair indicates swift messages and important information that will have a major impact on the surrounding situation.

## Jupiter

Jupiter is the king of the gods, an altogether bossy fellow, and attributed to the Wheel of Fortune. Never let it be said that this card couldn't overwhelm any other card in its vicinity. The planet Jupiter is the largest in our solar system and orbits the Sun in 11.8 years. It spends about a year in each sign and is retrograde approximately four to five months.

Jupiter rules change, expansion, growth, and development—ready or not. He revels in his powers in this regard and has a long memory. There is no stopping him when his temper is aroused—the lightening bolts carry his vengeance to those who defy his powers or supremacy. But Jupiter prefers to be connected with benevolence, mercy, generosity, good humor, and big-heartedness. He is sublime, enthusiastic, and prone to exaggeration. These are traits often seen in rulers, politicians, and strong leaders in any field who wish to be viewed favorably by the public. Jupiter is also connected with teachers, clergy, gurus, spiritual teachers, and healers.

Jupiter has two signs of rulership: Sagittarius and Pisces. In Sagittarius, we see his capacity for intellectual development; travel (by land or air); the historical growth of philosophy and religion (in civilization); personal ethics, faith, and spiritual development toward enlightenment. This sign encourages the Jovian pursuit of higher education and university degrees, as well as lengthy works requiring great dedication—books, symphonies, architectural achievements. In this sign, Jupiter encourages diplomacy and cooperation between nations (particularly through learning other languages). Thus, this may be considered the sign of ongoing cultural evolution that is brought about by inspired individuals. Jupiter fathered mortals who impacted the history of their times through their actions and quests. The Sagittarian Jupiter may be considered the historical Jupiter, the benefactor of outstanding individuals of any time period (whether heroic or notorious).

In Pisces, Jupiter is more spiritual and visionary, more boundless and keen on exploration of the unknown and unknowable. This aspect of Jupiter emphasizes travel by or over water, visits to sacred sites, cathedrals and temples, and places of healing such as hospitals and prisons. In these places, the spirit is compelled to grow while confined or limited in movement (consider the great works of literature produced by people in confinement or the enlightenment of Gautama Buddha that was occasioned by extended contemplation in stillness). The Piscean Jupiter emphasizes how the spirit can be free even when the body is trapped, thus leading to the mysteries of life after death and the powers that the forces of the universe have on the denizens of Earth. In this sign of extremes and paradoxes, Jupiter reveals the greatest heights of human nature, as well as its most degraded and deteriorated aspects: obliviousness, intoxication, delusion, and emotional manipulation through passivity, whining, tears, or blame.

In all ways, Jupiter is the supreme ruler of Olympus, and he never allows his subjects to forget this fact. Given Jupiter as an attribution, the Wheel carries this royal prerogative into the tarot. Life never stays the same—it's always changing (whether we can see it or not). Because of this planet's spiritual overtones, the life work, or karma, of a soul carries patterns into this life at birth and creates more patterns during the first twelve years of life (i.e. the first complete Jupiter cycle). These early patterns have an enormous impact on the subsequent life path, thus the Wheel has powerful karmic implications—what goes around comes around.

Jupiter is the chief executive in charge of the gods' influence on humanity. He can bestow great gifts, as well as terrible punishments for infractions. The spiritually ignorant individual may view events as blind fate; whereas the more spiritually developed person may have some understanding of the flow of his or her life's patterns and purpose. In any case, when the Wheel appears in a spread, it reveals a point at which these forces collide with the individual's life path, be it past, present, or future. Since the actual transit of Jupiter requires about a year in a sign, this card generally signifies a long-term effect in the works rather than a single incident of note. It is best to think of this card as a series of events that have brought about the necessity for changes in life, for growth or development beyond the current state. Troublesome patterns must be apprehended and transcended, or the pattern is likely to repeat.

The Wheel of Fortune is best buddies with the Temperance card (Sagittarius), and this combination indicates a highly developed spiritual awareness. The Moon card (Pisces) is also favorable with the Wheel in the sense of transcending the limits of physical containment and travel by water, but the Moon card has a difficult nature overall and needs to be favorably dignified by other cards in order for even the powerful Wheel to overcome her disagreeable attributes. The Wheel is also in good placement with the Chariot (Cancer), indicating travels of the mind or body that develop the soul. This card can indicate glitches with the Lovers (Gemini), a relationship with karmic overtones that demands growth for the partners involved. The Wheel is troubled near the Devil (Capricorn), as benefic Jupiter cannot like the limitations and evil traits of this card.

In the Minor Arcana, the King of Wands and the King of Cups demonstrate his earthly influence, embodying the traits of Jupiter in Sagittarius and Pisces, respectively. The five pip cards attributed to Jupiter (Eight of Swords, Six of Wands, Four of Swords, Two of Pentacles, and Nine of Cups) are magnified in proximity to the Wheel, increasing their impact on a reading. The Wheel provokes these cards to the extremes of their natural topics. For instance, the Wheel with the Six of Wands could be a noble winner or a sore loser. The Wheel is vulnerable to negative expression near cards with a Saturnian or Capricornian influence, as they provoke the harder aspects of fate and restrict methods for coping with it. In a spread with Judgment and/or the World, the Wheel signifies the compelling forces of destiny for the querent. Events at the time of the reading would be particularly significant, leading to accelerated maturity or learning in life.

## Mars

Mars, the red planet, is given in attribution to the Tower. An additional planet associated with the Tower is the transgenerational planet Pluto, which is notoriously disruptive. Mars is a god of war, known for his swift attacks, boldness, courage, and single-minded pursuit of goals. Ancient astrologers regarded this planet as *malefic* because of its propensity for destruction and chaos, danger, accidents, and violence. Yet Mars is a valuable fellow to have around—he's the warrior that serves the needs of the Sun (ego), a source of healthy root aggression, physical vitality, and the determination to break through to new ground. He also serves the desires of Venus by obtaining what she wants.

As in astrology, where Mars's range from useful aggression to senseless violence is dependent upon the favor or misfortune of placement in the chart, the Tower card's meaning varies with placement in a reading. The warrior god may be sophisticated or brutal, defending or demolishing. In the Tower, Mars spurs healthy struggles against smothering restrictions and traditions that are obsolete. In a most physical example, it's usually to the good when an old, decrepit building is torn down so a new building can be erected. As Mars is inconsistent in his relationships with other planets and zodiac signs, the Tower is equally inconsistent in spreads. This card may show the dread of destruction and collapse or the welcome invigoration of hard-won liberty; a reminder that liberty comes at a price and may require dangerous confrontations to acquire or restore. The Tower potently expresses upheaval in an individual's life, or the overthrow of an entire government, an individual reaction to personal violence or the collective reaction to violent events such as was experienced in September 2001.

The planet Mars rules Aries and Scorpio, the chief difference of expression being overtly aggressive behavior compared to covertly aggressive behavior. Both signs are passionate, sexually charged, and bent on gaining their deepest desires.

The orbit of this planet requires 687 days, slightly less than two years. Because of its reddish color, the planet is associated with heat, fire, fevers, bloody wounds, and violent illnesses. Mars retrogrades for a period of nearly three months at the end of each 1.5-year cycle.

Because Mars is so sensitive to sign and placement, cards neighboring the Tower can make or break the situation—just as Mars can be positive in taking the initiative to fulfill ambition or negative in impulsive haste and conflict. He can be defender or perpetrator. Likewise, the Tower can reflect inner awakenings that move a person's life in a new direction, or show havoc external to the person—oftentimes with bitter results. The Tower may be an explosion of sexual pleasure or the detonation of a bomb.

The Emperor (Aries) has a profound influence on the Tower, as he may be able to exert authority to contain the impact of destruction, directing it toward renewal of self-determination. The Death card (Scorpio) combined with the Tower is extremely potent and very seldom is a harbinger of good news. It may be positive in the sense that complete rebuilding is the result of total devastation. Mars exalts in Capricorn, so the Tower has an affinity for the Devil. Once again, the general motifs of these two cards are dark, and combined they may lead to evil, but the opposite spectrum of this combination may be a surprise pregnancy. It's important to note if the Tower precedes or follows these cards to determine the order of the situation. For example, if the Tower follows the Devil, it may represent gaining liberty from an oppressive situation or person. If the Tower is followed by the Devil, upheaval is followed by oppression or by unexpected new forms that manifest in the earthly potency of Capricorn—a new order subsequent to disorder.

Justice and the Hierophant are attributed to Mars's signs of fall (Libra) and detriment (Cancer). In these unfortunate dignities, a planet has to work harder to achieve its desired expression and results. Thus, the Tower has a short temper for the delicate negotiations of the Justice card and eschews the deliberate patience required by the spiritual disciplines of the Hierophant. The gentle, Venus-ruled Justice and Hierophant are far too aesthetic and cultured to make much with the Tower, which too often is like a wild animal that can't be tamed.

Because of Mars's propensity for evil or malefic manifestation, it's hard to make a case for the Tower's affinity with other cards. Again, card order is critical, and the Tower will assume its best meanings when followed by cards that allow for a healthy expression of ambition and courage (i.e., cards such as the Two of Wands, Six of Wands, and Three of Pentacles). Venus was able to calm Mars and manipulate him with her beauty, so the Tower in proximity to amenable Venus cards (such as the Seven of Cups) may mute the more violent connotations or encourage the Tower toward more noble motives (Four of Wands). The positive side of Mars, as a defender, champion, and idealist, is encouraged by proximity to the Emperor or Queen of Wands (both Mars-ruled Aries cards).

In the Tower, Mars the warrior may be blended with Pluto, Lord of the Underworld. This combination is an accurate attribution to the Tower, as Pluto rules explosions, eruptions, deadly danger, sabotage, and power battles that draw heated ferocity from the participants. Pluto is also the planet of transformation and rebirth—a quality often discovered in the rubble after a Tower-like incident occurs in a person's life. Pluto rules repressed or forgotten memories, buried in the subconscious mind, that may cause great shock to the conscious personality if they rise to the surface of awareness. Pluto is often connected with family dysfunction, incest, physical or emotional abuse, and evil manipulation. The Tower card often appears in spreads when this unfortunate circumstance exists for the querent, so the addition of Pluto to this card is useful for understanding the range and potential for violence inherent in this card.

Pluto acts like blind fate, unleashing circumstances with irrevocable impact on the life of the querent when aroused. This planet is extremely slow, as it orbits the outermost limits of our solar system. Its journey around the Sun requires 248 years, and its moon, Charon, is nearly half the size of the planet. They are locked into a mutual gravitational orbit, each always facing the other. The planetary orbit is irregular, and the planet spends roughly twenty years of its lengthy cycle inside Neptune's orbital path (most recently from 1978 to 1998). Pluto spends fifteen to twenty years in each sign, so its transits are powerful and its effects irreversible.

The Tower as ruled by Mars/Pluto has, therefore, a notable collective impact and may represent large groups of society and social organizations subject to disintegration. The reader must note if other planetary or zodiacal trumps are prominent in the reading, or if there is a concentration of Saturn or Jupiter cards. This would indicate that the querent's collective foundations are experiencing the impersonal forces of demolition, such as when an industry becomes obsolete or when a government is failing. The placement of the card, and its dignity, distinguishes the dominant forces at work on a case-by-case basis.

The image of the Tower is rooted in the concept of real estate, so its location in a spread is the primary way of determining its impact. Spread position will show if the card's meaning is focused on the inner life (bottom of a spread), the outer life (the top), or in events that are separate yet impact the life of the individual (spread positions that indicate the influence of others).

## Sun

The Sun card is attributed to the head honcho of the solar system and assumes primary stance with the other cards. All attributions must relate to him in some way: The Sun is the central source of light and energy, and is the primary symbol of the ego and the full achievement of personal potential. Our annual calendar is based on the daily motion of Earth as it orbits the Sun in 364.25 days—a terrene year. The Sun is associated with the gods Helios and Apollo in mythology. Helios was the charioteer, a titan, who guided the Sun on its daily journey across the sky following Aurora, the dawn. Phoebus Apollo was the Olympian sun god, the epitome of male achievement in sports, the arts, government, and all fine accomplishments. Apollo was a bachelor god, supposedly because he couldn't decide which Muse he desired. Vesta refused marriage to him, and in later myths he engaged in homosexual love relationships. He was the perfect son of Jupiter, understandably haughty and arrogant. His divine legacy to his children was the drive to succeed at all costs. Apollo couldn't bear being teased or made to look the fool, which is probably why his younger brother Mercury couldn't resist pushing his buttons. Two of his primary aspects in Greek civilization were as Delphic Apollo, god of the oracle, and as Apollo Delphinus, the god in the form of a dolphin. Sculptures of Apollo were meant to convey perfection of the nude male form, thus bringing the sculptor to the goal of divinely inspired artistic expression.

The Sun card glows with the positive accomplishments of Apollo and represents the full-flowering potential of the individual. The Sun is symbolic of the ego, and if well-dignified it may represent a fully integrated persona with mature self-awareness. It's a card with the best of all human qualities—nobility, graciousness, triumph, mastery of all tasks and difficulties. Solar light represents the divine potential within a human being. Fame, acclaim, talented children, and riches are the result of such Apollonian achievements.

In ill-dignity, the Sun card reverts to the more limited figure of Helios. This titan was accorded no relief from his daily task of guiding the chariot of the Sun across the sky, except for one disastrous time when his son by a mortal woman, Phaeton, took the reins. He was lost as the horses ran out of control, and he fell from the chariot. The hot Sun scorched parts of Earth past redemption, thus creating vast tracts of desert land. This is the potential malefic side of the Sun—the loss of a child, the deleterious effects of scorching heat, fevers, the excessive ego that rides roughly over others. These may be individuals who are bound to serving the relentless drives of their ego and can't be swayed from their course or their behavior, even for the well-being and safety of loved ones. This interpretation of the Sun is closely related to the Vedic understanding of the Sun as a malefic (which probably came about because India is subject to extremes of heat and drought). In ill-dignity, the Sun card may represent a person who is his or her own worst enemy because of stubborn resistance to growth and change.

Since the Sun is central to all the attributed planets (excluding the Earth's Moon), the planets benefit from his light. With Mercury (the Magician) the Sun prompts the highest forms of invention and communication. With Venus (the Empress) the Sun grants the fulfillment of desires and fruitfulness. With Mars (Tower), it launches a battle for preservation of identity or the development of a new persona from the wreckage of the old. With Jupiter (the Wheel) there is growth to a higher level of spiritual awareness and karmic fulfillment and the ability to illuminate the patterns at work. With Saturn (Judgment) the Sun reaches the outer boundaries of personal growth through time and regulates the timing of character tests one must face in the unfolding of the soul's evolutionary patterns.

The Sun must work toward balance with the High Priestess (Moon), a combination that implies the contrast between the conscious and unconscious mind. The Sun card will partake of any zodiacal or elemental attribute in the neighboring cards, expressing the range of that sign's strengths and weaknesses. For example, the Sun may lend a great deal of willpower when next to dreamy Seven of Cups, invigorating personal energy to see visions manifest in reality. With a difficult card like the Three of Swords, the Sun's light may bring the warmth of clear communication and harmonious efforts that dispel anxiety and fearfulness, or the strength of purpose to overcome sources of worry. The presence of the Sun card often reassures the others in its vicinity.

The Sun's court card is the Knight of Wands, who personifies the restless ambition and sheer vigor of the Sun-ruled sign Leo. The will to power and triumph is magnified by the Sun with the Strength card (Leo) but is prone to overestimation of personal strength and resources when in proximity to the Star card (Aquarius). The Sun will struggle near Justice (Libra), as ego-driven righteousness rarely has the detachment to evaluate legal issues with realism; the Sun and Emperor (Aries) combined deliver forceful drive, champions, and raw courage to surmount any struggle.

## Saturn

In many decks, the Judgment card depicts people rising from graves. The word *grave* is related to gravity, the underlying glue that keeps the solar system together. The alternate meaning for gravity is solemnity, a clear, deliberate view of the range of potential as an individual passes through a portal in life. If a person is being grave, he or she is being serious—a key word for Saturn. The Golden Dawn system attributes Saturn to the World card, as it symbolizes boundaries and limits of the manifestation of form. However, the divinatory meanings of the World card emphasize triumph and completion, and the card displays a picture of a woman dancing naked in space with Earth and the stars—ideas and images far too happy for grim Saturn. The symbolism and meanings of the Judgment card are a better fit for the qualities of Saturn as the Lord of Karma, tests of maturity, and finalities.

While GD die-hards and kabbalists are going to gnash their teeth over this attribution change, it does make for a very clean astrological correspondence. A full Saturn-Jupiter cycle, called a *mutation*, takes twenty years (XX Judgment), with the opposition occurring at the ten-year mid-point (X Wheel = Jupiter). A complete set of mutations in a single element takes two hundred years, totaling ten conjunctions at twenty-year intervals. Saturn is the backbone of time cycles on Earth, and historic collective turning points coincide with the Jupiter-Saturn conjunctions. These twenty-year cycles are measurements of cultural growth and decay, and this is most evident in economic cycles.

Saturn is the planet that rules form and containment. It demands a stark view of reality, relentless determination, and a commitment to long-term results. Saturn is the planet astrologers love to hate, because its lessons are often hard. But without underlying form, the brilliant visions of Jupiter would lack order or applicability, and the eloquence of Mercury would languish without poetic patterns and song forms into which the words and notes might be poured. We may see the elegant expression of poetry in the language skills of Mercury or the beauty of sentiment in Venus, but limericks, haiku, and Shakespeare's iambic pentameter are Saturnian forms that are the basis for the poetic craft. One may take this analogy to any skill of culture, or any tool of civilization. Jovian diplomacy would fail without Saturnian patience and prudence. A Venusian tapestry couldn't exist without the bonding agents in the thread dyes, the binding between the threads that create the substance of the fabric, or the hard, tensile surface of the needle that penetrates the fabric. It's impossible to embroider with a floppy noodle.

Where Jupiter overcompensates, Saturn undercompensates, represses, and feels fearful. This is the shadow side of Saturn, underlying self-defeating patterns conditioned in infancy and early childhood by parents, family, and the ambient culture. Saturn has a special set of fears in each sign of the zodiac: in Taurus, impoverishment; in Scorpio, impotence; in Capricorn, the parent or parental responsibilities, and so on. Fear is the counterpoint to enthusiasm in any important decision to be made: What if this choice leads to failure, bankruptcy, or a dead end?

This survey of Saturn gives a fuller understanding to the range of meanings possible with the Judgment card. Judgment demands awareness of pros and cons, a commitment to the hard work required to obtain results, and careful scrutiny of the precedents and history that predicate any decision.

When individuals make important life choices, they are exercising their authority, another key word for this planet. Some people are better prepared than others to approach the portals of life, and cards that are in proximity to the Judgment card will show the querent's capacity in this regard. In general, the more mature and wise a person is, the better his or her decisions will be. Maturity is what Saturn demands from its natives, and so equally does the Judgment card.

The neighboring cards of Judgment show which particular aspect of Saturn is going to be highlighted. For instance, with the High Priestess (Moon), the Judgment card may indicate a need to be aware of how emotions and unconscious or conditioned motives may influence a decision. The Emperor (Aries) with Judgment shows the full power of earthly authority as it manifests in government, law, and business, the potential for decisions to have a community impact. The Devil is attributed to Saturn's sign of rulership, Capricorn, and thus shares an important tie. Judgment may unleash the Devil's potential for fertile ambitions through an obsessive desire to succeed. The querent will need to confront the realities of the system at hand, the red tape and hurdles that must be surmounted to attain goals.

The Star card is attributed to Saturn's other sign of rulership, Aquarius. The Star and Judgment together may signal participation in a wave of the future, a shared vision of new development. The Strength card (Leo) should be a red flag for caution, as solemnity and passionate selfhood are not necessarily compatible partners in good decision making. The strength of the ego may unbalance the capacity for mature reflection, too self-absorbed to be cognizant of external limitations or overlying trends that may thwart achievement.

The Judgment card has another important facet connected with recognition on a collective level. While the individual may form judgments about his or her own life, in return, a society may form judgments about the value of an individual. A good example is a successful election campaign. A majority of citizens have acknowledged the individual's appropriateness to serve in a certain capacity and have granted public sanction for the candidate to perform a particular role in the structure of a community. If the person is particularly successful, history books may tell the stories of his or her accomplishments to succeeding generations—this is the legacy of Saturn. These functions carry over into the Judgment card and impute the potential for longevity and lasting results.

Judgment may also show that an individual has become aware of the causes and effects of his or her own past actions. Sometimes this can be a hard pill to swallow! The downside of this card is the potential for a sloppy attitude, a refusal to approach the next level of maturity in life lessons. Saturn demands patience and self-control and is the worst sort of bugbear if these traits are lacking. A spiritual path without discipline and commitment tempts fate to a dangerous degree. In this vein, cards that exemplify industriousness and the shouldering of responsibility will do quite well in proximity to Judgment. Lazy or fretful cards will exacerbate the harsher aspects of Judgment. Special attention should be paid to the pip cards attributed to Saturn (see page 92), as near Judgment these cards will reveal the fears or phobias that limit progress.

The two court cards that display Saturnian qualities are the Queen of Pentacles and the Knight of Swords. She is the stable earth mother, the rock and support of a family, the matriarch with the clout of parental authority. The Knight of Swords builds his ideas on the forms provided by Saturn. He moves with ease in developing a network of contacts within social hierarchies. Judgment has a particular affinity for the Two, Three, and Four of Pentacles (Capricorn), and these cards demonstrate the earthly process of development through maturity and careful planning. The three Aquarian pip cards, the Five, Six, and Seven of Swords, reflect some of the hardships and tests of Saturn, although the Six of Swords suggests the mastery of skills through discipline, and authority in the expression of talents.

A further facet of the Judgment card is that it shares an attribution to the element fire. The planet Saturn and the element fire are hard to reconcile on the surface. But Saturn rules things that feed, support, or contain fire—old growth trees, old souls, the spine that conducts the flow of kundalini,[13] the altar upon which a fire is burned. The pure spirit of fire is supported on a foundation of prior achievements in the Judgment card; thus history provides fuel for the forging of current and future events. History itself is a collection of the results of innumerable decisions. Yet when approaching the threshold of a decision, each individual must access the truth of his or her own inner spirit. The ability to keep the spiritual fires burning is tested at each successive level of development. As Saturn has a tendency toward inertia, the addition of the element of fire continually stimulates the impulse toward decision, the exercise of free will, and the impetus for self-determination.

Elemental fire provides light to see the pathway in the mind and the heart, burning away the structures and strictures of the past as the individual embraces the future. This combined attribution is apt when Judgment is functioning on a major collective level, as each generation is tested by the problems of its times. Saturn represents those things that are in the process of becoming obsolete, atrophied by time. Fire reduces those things to their primary components and rearranges them in a way that is more suited to the present and future.

•   •   •

The presence of planetary trumps in a spread is notable. One must consider how their divine prerogatives will impact their neighbors and whether one may expect a characteristic or erratic performance from these leading actors in the drama of life. The vagaries of script and set may be inferred from the attributions of neighboring cards, but only the actor himself can modulate the delivery of his performance in a scene.

--------

13 A Sanskrit word that translates to "fire serpent power." It is "shakti energy coiled like a sleeping serpent in a cavity near the base of the spine. When aroused . . . it ascends the central channel of the spine." (Omar Garrison, *Tantra: The Yoga of Sex*, New York: Julian Press, 1964, p. 235). The kundalini may be awakened through meditation practices or through the practice of tantric (sexual) yoga.

For readers who combine the tarot and astrology, an infinitely useful technique is to observe the actual planet(s) indicated in the querent's spread: in natal chart and by transit and progression. Faster planets reflect current and immediate events; slower planets reflect extended situations with a complex entwined history. The retrograde or direct stations of each planet are important timing elements, as are eclipses, as they are phenomena that display the relationship between the Sun, Moon, and Earth. Check contemporary eclipse dates if the Sun, Moon, High Priestess, or World appears in a spread.

# CHAPTER 7

# ELEMENTAL TRUMPS AND THE OUTER PLANETS

T he modern planets—Uranus, Neptune, and Pluto—were discovered after the invention of the telescope. Astrologers consider these planets agents of the collective, remote to the individual psyche and thus perpetrators of unpleasant manifestations on a personal level. The further the planet is from the Sun, the more erratic its orbit. The enigmatic energies of the planets from Saturn to Pluto are the least controllable for the individual ego.

The assignment of the outer planets to trumps adds depth to the delineation of the cards, as they provide archetypal models of behavior to cite. By deliberation or default, the outer planets have become associated with the elemental trump cards. Aleister Crowley assigned Uranus to the Fool (air) and Neptune to the Hanged Man (water) in his *Book of Thoth*. Pluto has been suggested as a "great awakener" for the Judgment card (fire), or as the "great destroyer" for the Tower card (Mars). Saturn is attributed to the World card (earth) by the Golden Dawn.

The following list provides optional placements for including Earth and the outer planets with the elemental trumps, but the choice is left to the discretion of the reader.

**Judgment:** fire, Saturn (or Pluto)

**Hanged Man:** water, Neptune

**Fool:** air, Uranus

**World:** earth/spirit, Earth

**Tower:** Mars (with Pluto or Uranus)

The outer planet assignments flesh out the purely conceptual influence of the elements. The airy Fool becomes the amoral Uranus, who revels in the fun of rebellion and unrestricted experimentation in the laboratory known as Earth. The submerged Hanged Man becomes Neptune, god of the ocean deep, personifying the depths of the unconscious mind—a realm without boundaries—and the sacrificial victim. Pluto is a raw force that rises from the depths to ignite the accelerant that explodes the Tower, or can be the painfully loud trumpet blast from the angel's horn that awakens the dead on the Judgment card.

World is Earth, the unity to which humanity belongs. Our home planet is a microcosm of the evolution of life in the universe. Gaia, the goddess who embodies the whole Earth, is depicted in the image of the woman dancing on traditional renderings of this card. She symbolizes the mingling of the four elements for survival and reproduction, and the symbiosis of all living things. The element of earth is united with the fifth element, spirit, to vivify all forms of life on the planet and to imbue its sentient life forms with the awareness of possibility.

A basis for using outer planets in tarot delineation is conferred by neighboring attributions. The Fool will have a more Uranian nature near the Star, the Emperor, or the Aquarian pips. The Hanged Man will be more Neptunian in proximity to the Moon and the Pisces pip cards, or near mutable mode cards. The Tower will be more distinctly Plutonian near Scorpio cards (Death, particularly) or may have a more evil expression when incited by Mars pip cards like the Nine of Swords.

The outer planets have no direct assignments to pip cards, but receive second-hand associations through the zodiac signs that they co-rule (see appendix A). This is just as well, because none of these godly characters are the type to invite to an afternoon tea party. Uranus, Neptune, and Pluto are unpredictable and uncontrollable, and their relevance is more clearly demonstrated in mundane, historic delineation. These planets impact the collective and can't be civilized, whitewashed, or made "politically correct" by any simple means. Where Saturn, the border lord, will represent standards one might in time achieve, the outer planets embody inexorable life circumstances one is compelled to live through, sometimes at the risk of survival. When bad things happen to good people, the three outer planets and Saturn are the usual suspects in astrology.

As elemental trumps, these cards will most clearly reveal the archetypal nature of the element near the Aces and Princesses of the four suits. The Fool near the Ace of Swords will indicate the impact of unexpected knowledge (airy thinking function) on the querent. The World will accentuate the successful establishment of material goals with the Ace of Pentacles through the earth-sensing function. Judgment with the Ace of Wands indicates births or awakening ambitions through the fiery intuiting function. The Hanged Man with the Ace of Cups represents the presence of powerful collective emotions that embody the watery-feeling function. When a Princess is near its related elemental trump, it suggests a person who is part of a collective experience of the elemental function. For instance, the Princess of Cups near the Hanged Man could represent a young woman who is mourning the death of a famous musician with many other fans.

The elemental trumps are generally well-dignified when placed near cards of the same (or compatible) element. One must keep in mind that well-dignified can mean that the card is most true to its divinatory meaning for good or bad. This would be the case if the Fool were placed near the Ten of Swords: the querent is likely to experience an unexpected and irrevocable ending, or may get a speeding ticket from a police officer hidden behind a blind curve. Elemental trumps are sensitive to their unfriendly elements. For instance, if the Hanged Man is next to the Five of Wands, the querent may feel lost in a competitive struggle. Neighboring cards affect the strength or weakness of the elemental trump cards and should be carefully monitored.

# CHAPTER 8

# PLANETARY AND ZODIACAL DIGNITIES

**Z** odiacal and planetary dignities are based on the attributions to the Major and Minor Arcana, and they lean heavily on the astrological rules for understanding relationships between the attributes. These dignities are specific refinements of the elemental dignities and add revealing subtleties to an interpretation. Knowledge of the relationships between signs and planets is needed to utilize these dignities.

## PLANETARY DIGNITY

Planetary dignity occurs when two pip cards share a planetary attribution or when pip cards are joined by their identical planetary trump card. When multiple cards attributed to a planet appear in a spread, it accentuates the force of the planet's characteristic qualities. The planet may also act as a primary influence in the behavior of neighboring court cards. (See also "Example 1" in chapter 4, page 37.) The predominance of Saturn-related cards have a profound effect on the overall interpretation of the spread.

Each of the planets is assigned to five pip cards, except Mars, which is given to six pips. The planets in the thirty-six decans of the zodiac follow Ptolemy's assignments,[14] and the pip cards numbered two through ten (thirty-six cards, with the four Aces as nascent element) are each assigned to one

---

14 Ptolemy's table of decan rulers is provided in William Lilly, *Christian Astrology* (1647; reprint, London: Regulus/Ascella Publications, 1985). There are other systems of decan rulerships available to astrologers and tarotists.

planet/decan set. The characters of the planets are thoroughly examined in chapter 6, "Planetary Trumps as Free Agents," and these descriptions will amplify the short introductions to each of the following groups of planetary attributions. The planet's dignity in the zodiac sign is given if appropriate: rulership and exaltation are forms of good dignity, while detriment and fall are forms of debility.

## Moon Pips

Partake of the lunar qualities of flux, liquidity, unconscious activity, influences from the past, feminine orientation and receptivity.

> **Six of Pentacles:** Moon/Taurus—*exaltation*
>
> **Four of Cups:** Moon/Cancer—*rulership*
>
> **Two of Swords:** Moon/Libra
>
> **Nine of Wands:** Moon/Sagittarius
>
> **Seven of Swords:** Moon/Aquarius

## Sun Pips

Partake of the solar qualities of individuality, pride, achievement, character, physical vitality, and capacity for joy.

> **Three of Wands:** Sun/Aries—*exaltation*
>
> **Ten of Swords:** Sun/Gemini
>
> **Eight of Pentacles:** Sun/Virgo
>
> **Six of Cups:** Sun/Scorpio
>
> **Four of Pentacles:** Sun/Capricorn

## Mercury Pips

Partake of the Mercurial qualities of communication, exchange, transfer, identification, dexterity, and linguistic and writing skills.

**Five of Pentacles:** Mercury/Taurus

**Three of Cups:** Mercury/Cancer

**Ten of Pentacles:** Mercury/Virgo—*rulership*

**Eight of Wands:** Mercury/Sagittarius—*detriment*

**Six of Swords:** Mercury/Aquarius—*exaltation*

## Venus Pips

Partake of Venusian qualities of pleasure loving, romanticism, desire orientation, beauty, attractiveness, valuation, and ornamentation.

**Four of Wands:** Venus/Aries—*detriment*

**Two of Cups:** Venus/Cancer

**Nine of Pentacles:** Venus/Virgo—*fall*

**Seven of Cups:** Venus/Scorpio—*detriment*

**Five of Swords:** Venus/Aquarius

## Mars Pips

Partake of the Martial qualities of aggression, dominance, goal-driven fervor, sheer physicality, and survival instincts.

**Two of Wands:** Mars/Aries—*rulership*

**Nine of Swords:** Mars/Gemini

**Seven of Wands:** Mars/Leo

**Five of Cups:** Mars/Scorpio—*rulership*

**Three of Pentacles:** Mars/Capricorn—*exaltation*

**Ten of Cups:** Mars/Pisces

## Jupiter Pips

Partake of the Jovian qualities of command, extension, expansion, wisdom, beneficence, free form development, spiritual growth.

**Eight of Swords:** Jupiter/Gemini—*detriment*

**Six of Wands:** Jupiter/Leo

**Four of Swords:** Jupiter/Libra

**Two of Pentacles:** Jupiter/Capricorn—*fall*

**Nine of Cups:** Jupiter/Pisces—*rulership*

## Saturn Pips

Partake of the Saturnian qualities of rigidity, bounded by limitations, form building, age and maturity, responsibility, fearfulness, and testing.

**Seven of Pentacles:** Saturn/Taurus

**Five of Wands:** Saturn/Leo—*detriment*

**Three of Swords:** Saturn/Libra—*exaltation*

**Ten of Wands :** Saturn/Sagittarius

**Eight of Cups:** Saturn/Pisces

## Predominance of Planetary Trump Cards

In addition to the predominance of a particular planet (or planets) shown by a spread's pip card attributions, planetary dignity is especially relevant when there is a predominance of planetary trump cards in a spread. The court and pip cards in the spread are most sensitive to the planetary trump in their zone. Another consideration is whether the planetary trumps are enhanced or challenged by the cards in their zone of influence—in other words, whether the environment is suitable for that planetary trump's overall meaning. The relative comfort of any planetary trump zones in a spread should be compared to each other. For example, if the Empress (which is generally thought to be a favorable card) is surrounded by troubling neighbors, it will be a Venus with thwarted desires. Conversely, neighboring court and pip cards whose attributions support the Martial potential for decisive transition may favorably enhance the generally disruptive influence of the Tower. These may include fiery cards or cards that offer a favorable zodiacal environment for Mars, such as Aries or Scorpio cards, or pips attributed to Mars that have a potentially victorious aspect, such as the Seven of Wands.

## ZODIACAL DIGNITY

The four element attributions of the suits are further subdivided into twelve zodiac signs. These are joined by the twelve zodiacal trumps and the cusp assignments of the court cards. Where planetary dignity implies a predominance of the planet's behavioral characteristics, zodiacal dignity implies environmental conditions and issues that are generated by the sign. Zodiacal dignity is most notable when pip cards are matched by the court card or zodiacal trump of their sign. An example of good zodiacal dignity is found in this card combination: Two of Swords, Justice, Four of Swords. Blended with the traditional meanings of the cards, the triple Libra (cardinal/air) attribution emphasizes the need for balance in partnerships and the ability to initiate negotiations and make decisions. Cards benefit when neighbored by cards with friendly zodiacal attributions as well—the earth and water signs are most compatible (Pentacles and Cups), as are the fire and air signs (Wands and Swords). Cards will also benefit when strengthened by a neighbor that shares its sign ruler (Aries and Scorpio, Taurus and Libra, Gemini and Virgo, Sagittarius and Pisces, Capricorn and Aquarius).

Zodiacal attributes are debilitated when neighboring cards share modality but not sign. Modalities are organized by crosses (quaternities) in the zodiac, and the signs at the axis points may be at cross-purposes. For example, the Three of Cups (Cancer/cardinal) will find the waffling of the Two of Swords (Libra/cardinal) quite irritating—fun isn't fun if it loses its spontaneity. Another example: the jubilant Six of Wands (Leo/fixed) loses some enjoyment of victories and positive momentum if placed near the worrisome Seven of Pentacles (Taurus/fixed).

Zodiacal attributions create a framework for determining planetary dignity. For example, the Ten of Cups (Pisces) next to the Wheel (Jupiter), the planetary trump whose attribution rules Pisces. This well-dignified combination emphasizes the spiritual and compassionate qualities of Pisces. Conversely, an ill-dignified zodiacal combination may occur when a planetary trump is surrounded by cards attributed to its signs of fall and/or detriment, for example, the combination Two of Pentacles, High Priestess, Five of Cups. The planetary trump of the Moon is bookended by Capricorn and Scorpio cards, her signs of detriment and fall. The High Priestess is suppressed and uncomfortable in this pip-card setting, unable to feel emotionally secure in a zone of unsettling change and uncertainty.

## EXAMPLES OF PLANETARY AND ZODIACAL DIGNITY ANALYSIS

The Cosmic Axis spread (see figure 10, Assertive Mars, on page 95) displays the Martial qualities of assertiveness and dominance. Numeric dignity is present in a pair of threes, and there is a preponderance of cardinal mode cards. The Three of Pentacles is in perfect dignity at the Midheaven Axis (Capricorn = natural tenth house). The underlying doubts of the Seven of Pentacles are well hidden by the aggressive confidence of the Emperor surrounded by two Mars pip cards and one Aries pip card.

A combination of fixed-mode cards; earth element; the sign of Taurus; its ruler, Venus; and its exalted planet, the Moon, present a spread with exceptionally good dignity between the cards (see figure 11 on page 96). This spread also contains a sequence of Five, Six, Seven. Although in the first and final cards, Venus is attributed to her sign of fall (Virgo) and detriment (Scorpio), the surrounding Taurus cards and the shared planetary dignity between the Seven of Cups and the Nine of Pentacles leverage these challenging Venus attributions into a pleasant expression of her characteristics, particularly

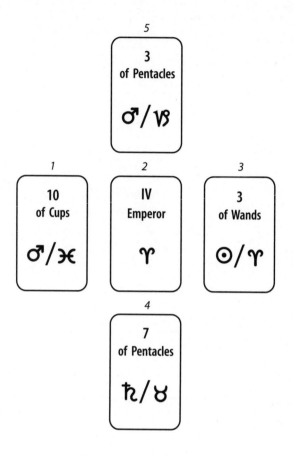

*Figure 10: Assertive Mars*

Card 1: Ten of Cups—Mars/Pisces, mutable

Card 2: Emperor—Aries (ruled by Mars), cardinal

Card 3: Three of Wands—Sun/Aries, exalt, cardinal

Card 4: Seven of Pentacles—Saturn/Taurus, fixed

Card 5: Three of Pentacles—Mars/Capricorn, exalt, cardinal

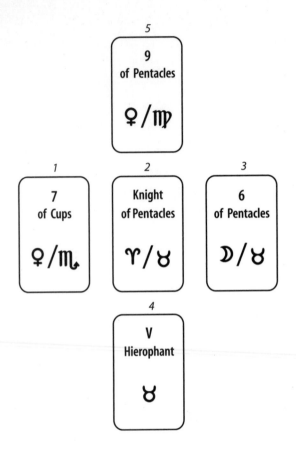

Figure 11: Well-Dignified Venus

Card 1: Seven of Cups—Venus/Scorpio, detriment, fixed

Card 2: Knight of Pentacles—Aries/Taurus cusp, fixed

Card 3: Six of Pentacles—Moon/Taurus, exalt, fixed

Card 4: Hierophant—Taurus, fixed

Card 5: Nine of Pentacles—Venus/Virgo, fall, mutable

in her earthy Taurean qualities of material gain and comfort, highly valued skills, and sensual pleasure.

. . .

Zodiacal and planetary dignities may be separated in theory, but as shown in the above examples, they can't be separated in practice. The planetary dignities (signs of rulership, exaltation, detriment, and fall) are discussed in chapter 6, "Planetary Trumps as Free Agents," in the sections about each planet. In addition, a quick reference chart is in appendix C.

# CHAPTER 9

# THE COSMIC AXIS AND OTHER SPREADS

O ne of the most common tarot spread forms is in the shape of a cross, two axes that intersect at a central axle card. The cross is an ancient symbol, energy pattern, glyph, or rune expressing the tremendous dynamic that occurs when a rising line meets and becomes aware of a horizontal line.

Two primitive examples of crosses and their symbolism are the runes that are shaped like crosses.

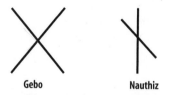

Gebo                     Nauthiz

*Figure 12: Cross-Shaped Runes*

Gebo shows the two lines meeting in harmony and balance. This cross has positive energy and represents union, meetings, decisions, and sex. The second rune, Nauthiz, is an asymmetrical cross that shows tension, anxiety, urgency, and need. This axis is the cross of necessity.

When two lines meet, some sort of exchange or manifestation is implied. This is amply demonstrated in astrological chart forms, as the Ascendant/Descendant horizon axis is intersected by the Midheaven/Nadir vertical axis.

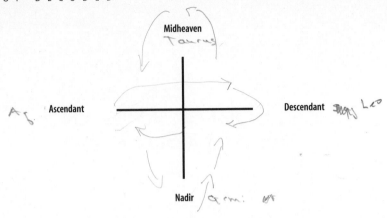

*Figure 13: The Cosmic Axis*

This axis can be considered a cosmic compass. The first point on the horizon, the Ascendant, represents the individual: the self, the window of perception, the body that contains the current incarnation. The opposing point of the horizontal axis is the Descendant, which represents the other: the partner or spouse, one-on-one relationships, the content and impact of intimacy, and the mutual influence exchanged during encounters with other individuals.

The vertical axis is defined at the bottom by the Nadir (also called the IC, an abbreviation for the Latin, *Imum Coeli*, or lower heaven). This axis point represents the roots and origins, the family, the genetic tree of the individual, the history of the family, and the beginning and ending of life. The Midheaven (also called the MC, the *Midi Coeli* or middle heaven) is at the top of the axis. This point represents the direction the life will take as the individual moves out into the world. This includes the things in the environment that shape a path, including work, authority figures, expectations, and the parameters that encourage or limit achievement.

Every symbol, glyph, or rune has a pattern of vitality that is determined by the flow of energy through the lines that compose the symbol. It's important to think about the way the energies flow through the Cosmic Axis. The horizon line's energy moves from left to right and back again. The vertical axis flows from bottom to top and then returns to the bottom. As the lines meet in the center, there is a dynamic interaction between all four axis points. This *axle point* is the mixing bowl, because it partakes of the influences of the whole.

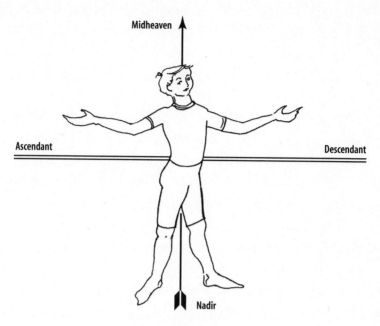

*Figure 14: Axis Boy*

Carl Jung utilized the cross glyph as the symbol to embody the concept he called the *quaternity,* the perfect balance of four that resolves the dynamic tension of a trinity. The horizontal line is termed the *axis of encounter,* and the vertical line is the *axis of differentiation.*[15] This is quite similar to the astrological model: the horizontal Ascendant/Descendant axis shows the polarity between the self and others, how the self reaches outward to act and react with others, and returns to the inner self to evaluate the impact of the exchange. The vertical MC/IC axis shows the energy of the soul rising from unknown depths into a family, community, and nation of origin; a soul rooted in a specific collective conscious and unconscious that rises to encounter the world and sinks back to its origins to reflect and recuperate. The axis of differentiation rises through the axis of encounter to point the way into the world at large, with the ultimate purpose of fulfilling individual potential

---

15 Carl Jung, *The Archetypes and the Collective Unconscious* (Princeton: Princeton Univ. Press, 1969), 233–242.

within the collective. How this is fulfilled is a co-function of origin, differ-entiation, and relating (the development of the individual through the three lower points, or trinity), and it is enacted in the environment as the indi-vidual strives to find a role that both serves the group and provides opportunities for survival and fulfillment.

Additional useful information can be found by further discussion of the astrological chart form. Think of the axis overlaid on the body of a human—personified here as Axis Boy (see figure 14 on page 101). Axis Boy's extended arms follow the path of the Ascendant/Descendant axis. The right hand needs to know what the left hand is doing. His feet are placed on the ground at the Nadir, showing his connection to Earth and his roots. His head is the Midheaven, demonstrating how he has to use his noggin effec-tively to get along in the world.

The Cosmic Axis has four hemispheres and four quadrants, as shown in figure 15. The horizon line divides the space into a lower (north) and upper (south) hemisphere: the inner self and the outer self. The vertical line divides the space into a left (east) and right (west) hemisphere: the individual and the other. The four quadrants are as follows: the first quadrant represents the development of self; the second represents growth as it is influenced by the family environment, friends, and learning. The third quadrant concerns inter-actions through relationships that may take place at many levels, and the fourth represents the results of the prior three quadrants.

The directions on this axis are a reversal of what is normally seen on a compass, with north occupying the top position. The astrological compass is different because of the manner in which Western astrologers graphically depict the zodiac in a counter-clockwise order around a circle. In a natural zodiac chart that features Aries at the Ascendant, the "northern signs" occupy the bottom half of the chart. This orientation is retained for all charts. For taro-tists, knowledge of the reversed compass orientation of the Cosmic Axis is useful if the spread is being used to locate missing objects or people, or to forecast the direction of travel.

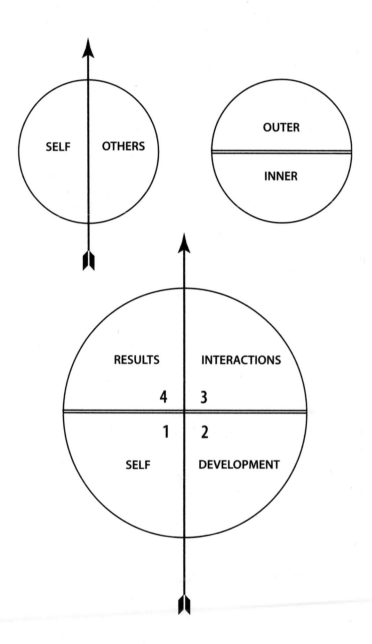

*Figure 15: Hemispheres and Quadrants*

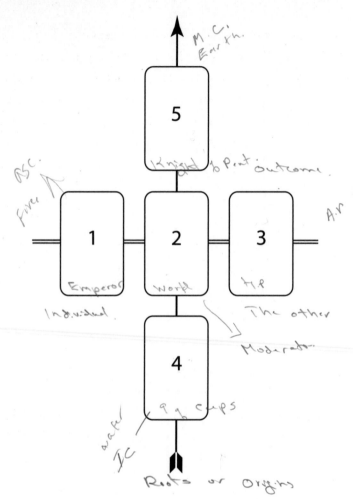

*Figure 16: Cosmic Axis Spread*

## THE COSMIC AXIS SPREAD

The Cosmic Axis spread requires five cards. In keeping with the astrological model, card 1 represents the individual, and card 3 represents the other. Card 4 signifies the roots or origins, and card 5 is the destination or outcome. Card 2 in the center (the axle) acts as a moderator between the four axis-point cards.

As with choosing a significator card, Jung's four functions, intuiting, feeling, thinking, and sensing, are also acceptable to use for position meanings as a variation on the astrological axis meanings. As shown in the list below, these functions are placed in polarity to their natural elemental counterparts in Jung's schema and are correlated further to relate to the natural zodiac rulers of the axis points. (Some authors switch the elemental assignments to thinking/fire and intuiting/air.)

**Intuiting:** Aries, Ascendant, fire

**Feeling:** Cancer, IC, water

**Thinking:** Libra, Descendant, air

**Sensing:** Capricorn, MC, earth

There is a remarkable correspondence of meaning between the astrological axis points and Jungian quaternity that compounds the interpretational potential of the spread. A sixth cover card may be drawn and placed over card 2 in the central position to complete the reading.

If more cards are needed or desired, the Cosmic Axis spread is easily expanded. The Cosmic Axis is the skeleton for the Twelve-House layout, and the next layout is an abbreviated version of the full Twelve-House spread.

## THE VALA CROSS

This spread (shown on page 106) is an expanded adaptation of the Cosmic Axis spread. It requires twelve or thirteen cards, your choice. Review the information on hemispheres and quadrants (figure 15) to derive additional understanding of the flow of this arrangement.

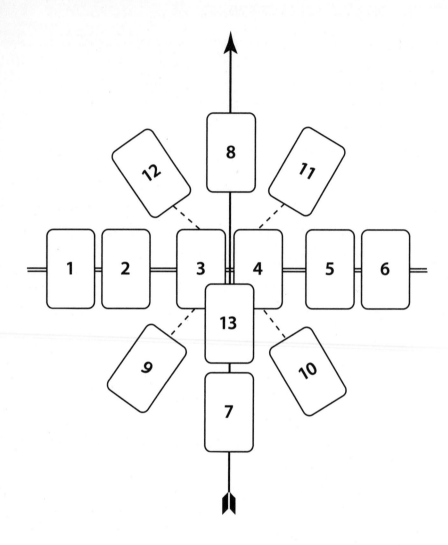

*Figure 17: The Vala Cross Spread*

The card position meanings as shown in figure 17 are as follows:

**1 and 2:** The individual, past circumstances

**3 and 4:** Current situation, heart of the matter

**5 and 6:** Significant others who affect the situation, their condition and mood

**7:** Roots, origin, family, past elements that affect present situation (cards 3–4)

**8:** Direction of future movement; the career, authority figures, important activities and actions

**9:** Money and daily life for the individual (corresponds to the first quadrant)

**10:** Children, creativity, love, work and coworkers (second quadrant)

**11:** Shared money and resources, transitions, beginnings, and endings (third quadrant)

**12:** Desired results, external factors that may affect future, concealed issues (fourth quadrant)

**13:** A final thirteenth card may be drawn to cover the central cards 3 and 4 as a summation or final outcome card.

In this spread, the axis of encounter has been doubled—a second cross diagonally intersects the upright cross. This expands the descriptions of the querent's situation and delineation of a question. Further, the pairs found along the horizontal axis provide extra details about relationship questions.

The general guidelines of the energy patterns for an axis-related spread apply here: follow the flow of energy between cards 1 through 6 and back again, and then along the vertical axis of card 7, cards 3–4 (central pair), and card 8, returning to the bottom. Observe the exchange of energies between the cards in the quadrants, which form a second axis in the spread—from card 9 to 11, and between cards 10 and 12. Cards 3–4 (and this would include cover card 13) moderate the dialog between these axis points.

Take a look at the hemispheres as well. Cards 9, 7, and 10 are the lower hemisphere and will show a great deal about the querent's inner, private life. Cards 12, 8, and 11 are the upper hemisphere and show elements that are in the querent's outer, public life or what will be encountered there in the future. The left hemisphere consists of cards 1–2, 9, and 12, and these cards show what the querent can provide or access on his or her own initiative. The right hemisphere consists of cards 10, 5–6, and 11 and show what must be obtained through negotiations and agreements with others and the impact others may have on the individual.

## THE TWELVE-HOUSE SPREAD

This traditional spread mimics a full horoscope chart format. The cards explain and describe matters related to each house. In astrology, the houses are inconstant—they are always moving and revolving, and (depending on the type of house system used) they may not always contain the same number of degrees from house to house. Actually, houses are an arbitrary system that is superimposed on the zodiac, subdividing it in a way that is useful for interpretation. The signs of the zodiac, on the other hand, are always consistent and measured in thirty-degree segments.

Where the Vala Cross has two intersecting crosses, the Twelve-House spread has three intersecting crosses. Still, the cross of primary importance is the horizontal-vertical axis. The cards that occupy these placements are always of the greatest importance.

Card position meanings are:

**First House (Ascendant):** The self, modes of perception, general demeanor of the individual

**Second House:** Skills, abilities, capacity to earn a living, possessions, and personal values

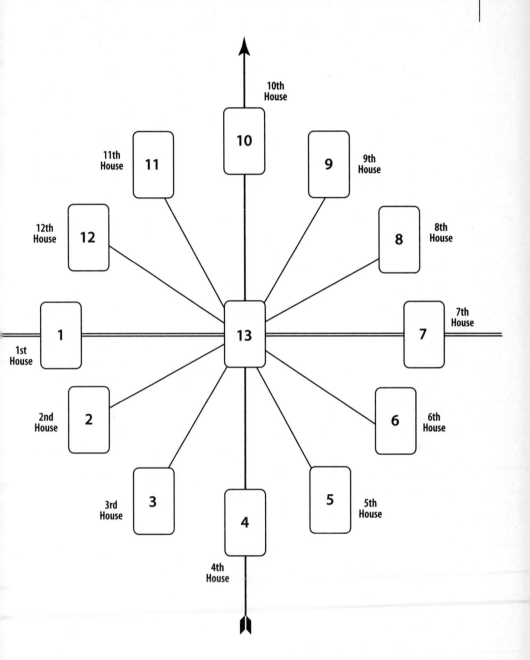

*Figure 18: The Traditional Twelve-House Spread*

**Third House:** Daily life, siblings, short journeys, discussions

**Fourth House (Nadir/IC):** Inner life, family, origins, private thoughts and feelings, past foundations

**Fifth House:** Creativity, children, love affairs, the ability to express the ego's contents

**Sixth House:** Work, health, coworkers, issues the individual must work through with others

**Seventh House (Descendant):** Relationships, transactions, agreements, marriage partner

**Eighth House:** Shared resources with spouse or partners, transitions with family or spouse

**Ninth House:** Education, spiritual and intellectual matters, long-term plans

**Tenth House (Midheaven/MC):** Career, bosses, life path, future direction, conditions in the real world

**Eleventh House:** Group associations, desired results, hopes for the future

**Twelfth House:** Areas lacking access or control: confinement, illness, blind spots, family issues that may besiege or haunt the querent.

A thirteenth card may be drawn to place in the center as a summation card. This final card will act as a moderator between all six axis pairs. The reader may choose to place the central card first and follow around the houses—one through twelve with cards 2 through 13.

The cards are read through the natural flow of energy between axis points of the three crosses contained in this spread. The Cosmic Axis (first, fourth, seventh, and tenth houses) is the axis of predominant importance. In a Twelve-House spread, the Cosmic Axis is also the *cardinal axis,* because the natural signs on these four points are all cardinal signs. The secondary cross is the *fixed axis,* consisting of the second, fifth, eighth, and eleventh houses. The final cross is the *mutable axis,* consisting of the third, sixth, ninth, and twelfth houses.

Although it is useful to read the cards sequentially as spread, around the circle counterclockwise from the first to the twelfth house, much more meaning can be derived by reading the opposing pairs of the three quaternities contained in this spread. Begin by comparing the Ascendant/Descendant axis, the first and seventh houses (as moderated by the center card, of course) and work through the oppositions, with the second and eighth houses next, and so on. Observe the houses by hemispheres and quadrants for additional meaning and blending of card energies.

## THE ZODIAC SPIRAL SPREAD

This is a much more complex method for spreading the cards, but the results are worth the effort. It requires eighteen cards, as shown in figure 19 on page 112, and the cards are placed in a substantially different manner than the simpler Twelve-House spread.

Observe this pattern of spreading the cards carefully. Notice how it still looks very much like a Twelve-House spread. Instead of placing the cards sequentially around the circle of houses, they are spread in the order of the three crosses that occur in a Twelve-House arrangement. The additional five cards cover the four Cosmic Axis points (the cardinal axis) and the first, central card. The house meanings in the Zodiac Spiral remain essentially the same as in the Twelve-House spread—it's only the ordering of placement that differs. Expanded meanings are given below, however, since this is a more advanced layout than the Twelve-House spread.

**Card 1, Center:** The person's soul, will, intentions.

**Card 2, First House:** Attitude toward past and present. How the querent views current experience. Body and personality—strengths and weaknesses.

**Card 6, Second House:** Stable elements—past and present. Long-term emotions, situations; talents, abilities, earnings, values, possessions, nourishment.

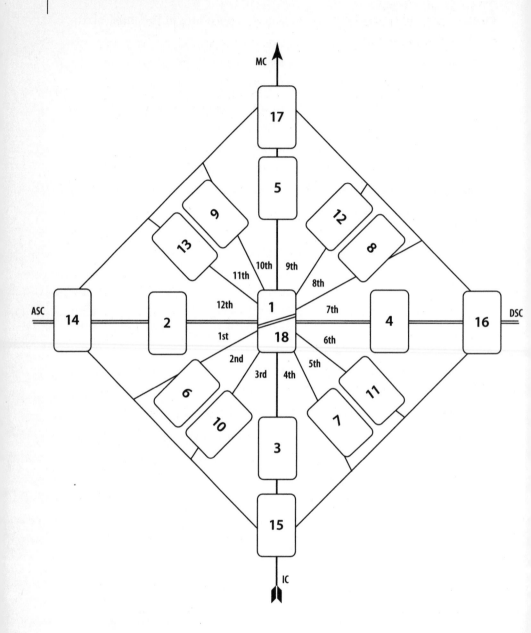

*Figure 19: The Zodiac Spiral Spread*

**Card 10, Third House:** Changing elements, things in flux. Conditions to problem/question; causes of change. Recent past. Thoughts, ideas, discussions.

**Card 3, Fourth House:** Basis of question—motivation, inner goals, and desires. Home, family, dwelling place, beginnings, and endings. Origin.

**Card 7, Fifth House:** Desires, ideas, love, and ego. Risks. Defines the question or concern, the person's expectations. Children and friends.

**Card 11, Sixth House:** Problems and obstacles, past and present. Distractions. Conditions to be considered for improvement. Work and coworkers. Issues to work through. Health and well-being, stamina. Analysis.

**Card 4, Seventh House:** Present status. That which is coming in. Relationships, partners, contracts and agreements. Allies and enemies.

**Card 8, Eighth House:** Results and conditions of seventh house—transformations in environment, attitudes, emotions, attachments. Partner's needs and skills. Actions needed to change or transform situation/question.

**Card 12, Ninth House:** Suggested strategies, big picture. What needs to be learned or unlearned. Sources of help, teachers, journeys. Ultimate goal.

**Card 5, Tenth House:** That which can be achieved. Future trends and direction.

**Card 9, Eleventh House:** Future outlook, short-term. Any radical changes. Adjustments required by tenth-house card. Friends.

**Card 13, Twelfth House:** Long-term future. Spiritual and inner development. Obstacles or unexpected future conditions. Work to be done.

## Final Cover Cards:

**Card 14, Ascendant:** Future personal development.

**Card 15, IC:** Inner strength, family and home, foundation of the future.

**Card 16, Descendant:** Future transactions, opportunities through relationships and allies, or problems from enemies.

**Card 17, Midheaven:** Summation, ultimate achievement, directions.

**Card 18, Center:** Growth of will, intentions, changing views and personality. Personal development—that which should be cultivated.

Analyze the spread by house content and then by comparing cards with axial relationships. Review the inhabitants of the four hemispheres and four quadrants. The cover cards give additional emphasis to the Cosmic Axis within the spread and should be related to the final, central axle card (card 18). The reader should consider elemental and modal dignity, numeric dignity, and the impact of the planetary trumps if they appear in the spread. Finally, there is the consideration of locational dignity, the subject of the next chapter.

# LOCATIONAL DIGNITIES

A technique that blends cartomancy and occult attribution systems is *locational dignity*. Locational dignity occurs when a card, by its divinatory meaning, numeric designation, or attribution, appears in an appropriate or inappropriate location in a spread. Some forms of this type of dignity are very simple and easily discerned, while other forms require in-depth knowledge of spread forms and attribution systems.

The simplest form of locational dignity is a card sharing the number of its position—for example, the Two of Cups in the second position in the spread. Both the numeric vibration and the assigned meaning of the spread position are emphasized in this case. Trump and pip cards all have numeric designations and may appear in positions that match their number.[16]

Cartomantic, or meaning-based, locational dignity is applicable to all card layout arrangements and occurs when the card's divinatory meaning blends favorably with its position meaning. For example, if a querent inquires about the future outcomes of a business deal, the Ten of Pentacles would be well-dignified in the outcome position because it suggests wealth and long-lasting results. The Lovers card in a relationship position is well-dignified in a question about romance.

Both numeric and meaning-based locational dignities, however, are subject to scrutiny of the neighboring cards, which may either support or

---

16 The numbers assigned to the court cards are as follows: Kings = 2, Queens = 3, Knights = 6, and Princesses = 10. Aleister Crowley, *The Book of Thoth* (Stamford, CT/New York: U.S. Games Systems, 1969), 268.

hinder the dignity of location. Neither of these forms of locational dignity is very strong, and they rely on the support of neighboring cards.

## ASTROLOGICAL ATTRIBUTIONS

The astrological attributions constitute an extended and specific form of locational dignity applicable to the Cosmic Axis and Twelve-House spreads. These attributions are evaluated by comparing the location of the cards to the natural planetary and zodiacal rulers of each axis point and by correlating the twelve houses with the cards that occupy those positions in the spread. For example, if Judgment appears in the tenth house (or on the MC axis), the card gains enormous strength by being placed in Saturn's location of greatest authority. This method blends the dignities of astrology and tarot by merging the spread form with the Twelve-House format (as detailed in chapter 9).

The locations of good dignity for the Major Arcana in the twelve houses are as shown in table 3, which appears on page 117.

Three of the elemental trumps (with their optional planet attributions) become unusually strong in their locations of dignity. The Fool (Uranus/air) and the Hanged Man (Neptune/water) exhibit double dignity in their houses, as they are attributed to both the element and the ruling planet of the house. The Judgment card finds good dignity on three of four points of the Cosmic Axis: It triumphs on the Ascendant because of its fire attribution; it triumphs on the Descendant Axis because Saturn exalts in Libra (natural seventh-house sign); and finally, Judgment attains perfect dignity on the Midheaven Axis because Saturn rules Capricorn (the natural tenth-house sign). The Judgment card is quite ill-dignified in the fourth house (or Nadir position), as Saturn is in detriment in this house, unfriendly with its ruler, the Moon, and fire is the adversary of water, this house's natural element.

Perfect dignity is attained when a card is placed in a position that perfectly matches its attributes. It should be noted that *a card in perfect dignity will display its most exact divinatory meanings, for good or for evil.* For example, Death (Scorpio) in the eighth-house position is in perfect dignity, and this placement also exhibits the Death card's most extreme meanings: death,

**Table 3: Locational Dignity for the Major Arcana**

| House | Sign/Ruler/Element-Exalted | Trump |
|---|---|---|
| First | Aries, Mars, fire, Sun | Emperor, Tower, Judgment, Sun |
| Second | Taurus, Venus, earth, Moon | Hierophant, Empress, World, High Priestess |
| Third | Gemini, Mercury, air | Lovers, Magician, Fool |
| Fourth | Cancer, Moon, water, Jupiter | Chariot, High Priestess, Hanged Man, Wheel |
| Fifth | Leo, Sun, fire | Strength, Sun, Judgment |
| Sixth | Virgo, Mercury, earth | Hermit, Magician, World |
| Seventh | Libra, Venus, air, Saturn | Justice, Empress, Fool, Judgment |
| Eighth | Scorpio, Mars and Pluto, water | Death, Tower, Hanged Man |
| Ninth | Sagittarius, Jupiter, fire | Temperance, Wheel, Judgment |
| Tenth | Capricorn, Saturn, earth, Mars | Devil, Judgment, World, Tower |
| Eleventh | Aquarius, Saturn and Uranus, air | Star, Judgment, Fool (double dignity) |
| Twelfth | Pisces, Jupiter and Neptune, water, Venus | Moon, Wheel, Hanged Man (double dignity), Empress |

destruction, inheritance, and regeneration. A spread with more than one card in perfect dignity is exceptional.

In the Cosmic Axis spread, four planetary trumps rule the four axis points. The ruler of the natural[17] Ascendant is Mars, or the Tower card. This is raw

17 The "natural ruler" is the planet ruling the sign that naturally occurs on that particular axis. Aries is the natural Ascendant, Cancer the natural IC, Libra the Descendant, and Capricorn the MC.

life energy that first arrives as a living, breathing baby made of bone, muscle, skin, and organs, with a set of potentials for growth, personality, ability, and survival skills. The ruler of the Nadir (or IC) is the Moon, or the High Priestess card. Here we see the flow of blood through the baby that stretches back through uncounted generations. The High Priestess provides a specific set of genetic characteristics, a family environment, imprinting, bonding, and conditioned behaviors that influence a child's growth. This card also represents the underpinning of the collective unconscious that resides within each baby, as well as his or her own individual unconscious.

The Descendant is ruled by Venus, the Empress. Here the individual finds the pleasures and dangers of intimacy through one-on-one relationships. These are experiences that are common to all humans, but since each person is unique (the Ascendant), he or she will initiate, react to, and perceive interactions in unique ways. Here is where individuals learn about human nature and about their own nature through reflecting on how their desires and values compare with those of others. Either they will obtain their wants and needs from relationships with others, or they won't. A learning curve is achieved over time, yet success is not guaranteed.

Finally, Saturn, the Judgment card, rules the Midheaven. It is here that the individual meets the structures, hierarchies, rules, powers, and limitations of the collective. The individual must constantly make choices, or judgments, about how to best operate in the world as he or she finds it. Maturity is a necessity for development. Ideally, the individual gains authority with age, with various characteristic personality traits, attitudes, and mannerisms being molded by experience and solidified around the age of twenty-eight (the first Saturn return). This authority should continue to grow and develop until a person reaches his or her mid- to late fifties, during the second Saturn return. During this period the individual begins to release earthly power and responsibilities for work and family, and moves toward the quiet and introspective period of retirement. This Saturnian pattern is an idealized model of development, so the response of each individual will manifest in singular ways.

If the planetary trumps ruling the axis points are positioned at their own axis, they are in perfect dignity and have a tremendous influence on the reading as a whole. The axis with its own ruler becomes a focal point in the spread, and the area of life indicated by the axis is infused with tremendous energy and activity. Any card on the Cosmic Axis gains importance, but the freewheeling planetary trump axis rulers magnify the area of life designated by that axis, and the highlighted axis is being enacted in the querent's life through the archetypal models or behavior patterns. The zodiacal trumps ruling these four axis points also receive excellent dignity when placed on their axis points: Emperor (Aries) at the Ascendant, Chariot (Cancer) on the Nadir, Justice (Libra) on the Descendant, and the Devil (Capricorn) on the MC.

Not all of the pip cards can attain perfect dignity. For example, while the Two and Three of Wands both attain perfect dignity in the first house, the Four of Wands is attributed to Venus, who is in detriment in Aries (and in the first house). The Four of Wands is in good dignity in the first house as an Aries card and in good dignity in the seventh house as a Venus card, but neither location will confer perfect dignity on this card because of the conflicting attribution. Examine the lists of pip cards given in chapter 8, "Planetary and Zodiacal Dignities," to see which cards have been given an attribution of ill-dignity, that is, a planet in its sign of fall or detriment. These cards will never find perfect dignity, but may experience good dignity in the houses that match either the zodiacal attribution or the planetary attribution, and they will also be moderately well placed in houses that share the same suit element.

Cards may become ill-dignified when they are placed in the house opposite from their natural location. Planetary trumps will struggle in their signs/houses of detriment and fall (outlined in appendix C). Depending on the relevant dignities of neighboring cards shared with the planetary trumps in an ill-dignified location, the planetary trumps may be assisted or further debilitated. A debilitated planetary trump exhibits the most difficult characteristics of its planet and divinatory meanings; thus the querent struggles to attain the typical priorities of the planet/card as it would be experienced in a good position.

Other spread forms unrelated to the Cosmic Axis may be interpreted by aspects of locational dignity, but this is more of a matter of common sense and knowledge of the nature of the cards. Certain cards will thrive in specific positions. For instance, the World card will generally have its most positive dignity when it appears at the center of a spread, and the Sun shares this dignity. The logic behind this dignity is that the Earth (World) is the center of gravity for humans, and the Sun is the center of the solar system. Mars and Saturn are considered to be malefic planets, and the cards attributed to these planets will function very well (that is, in their most characteristic manner) in an external or result-producing position of a spread. Cards of triumph, like the Six of Wands, Nine of Cups, Temperance, and the four Aces are also well placed in outcome positions. Likewise, soft, feminine, domestic cards like the Empress, the Three of Cups, the Six of Cups, the Six of Pentacles, and the Queen of Cups, perform well in positions that have meanings related to family condition and inner self, or to romantic relationships.

The Magician and the High Priestess merit separate consideration. Their attributed planets, Mercury and the Moon, represent perception (intake) and exchange (output), the immediate response of the senses and mind. These functions define the composition of the individual's reality and symbolize the basic parameters of consciousness. They enjoy the best dignity when placed in their houses of natural rulership and exaltation. Yet because of the velocity of the two planets represented, their placement in any location is notable, suggesting that the area of life (house) is being enlivened, animated by exchanges (Magician) or great changes in emotions (High Priestess). If these two cards are neighbors, the essences of immediacy and response are at hand. The quality of the querent's absorption and response, with keen alertness to emotional shifts, is being exercised. The neighbors and position of this pair will indicate where this activity is most intense and with whom it's likely to occur.

If either Magician or High Priestess appears on an axis, the process of the axial exchange is magnified. The card placed at the opposite axis indicates the focus and impact. For example, if the Magician is at the Nadir of the Cosmic Axis, and the Five of Pentacles is at the Midheaven, the impulse or necessity to communicate effectively with the outer world is being hampered. The Five of Pentacles is attributed to Mercury/Taurus, so with the

Magician at the Nadir the inner need to have forward momentum in transactions is being thwarted by delays, lack of money, absence of significant individuals, dishonesty, or misunderstandings about end results. The querent should be very clear about goals and patient for results, as conflicting issues in the environment may confuse his or her perceptions (Mercury).

• • •

When attribute-based locational dignity is related to the Cosmic Axis and Twelve-House type spreads, it forms a basis for a detailed evaluation of placement. This method may be extended to apply to the querent's horoscope as the houses of a card spread are compared with the houses of the chart. Although this combined spread-chart analysis may seem remote, it was a technique developed and written about by Etteilla in the 1780s. This pioneering tarotist created a method of erecting a horary chart from a tarot spread, derived from a set of astrological attributions to the cards. The chart is interpreted with the rules of astrology.[18] Etteilla's method also utilized cartomantic analysis in the instructions for his spread, making it apparent that he advocated an equal respect to both "card smarts" and the use of astrological dignities.

The delineation of a Twelve-House type spread using the rules of astrological locational dignity is a lengthy process for the reader. Fluency in this method requires persistent effort and memorization. A complete Twelve-House graph of cards in the location matching their natural house-related attributions (good dignity) is presented in appendix F in a horoscope chart format.

18 Found in Etteilla's book, *Manière de se récréer avec le jeu de cartes nommées tarots (How to Have Fun with the Deck of Cards Called Tarot)* (Amsterdam and Paris: Segault & Legras), 1785. See also: E. Hazel and J. Revak, "The First Systematic Integration of Tarot and Astrology: Etteilla's Correspondences and Divinatory Method," which first appeared in *The Tarot Journal* 2, no. 1 (spring 2002): 15–31, and is now available at *www.villarevak.org/astro/main.html*.

# CHAPTER 11

# DIRECTIONAL SCANNING

**D**irectional scanning[19] is a physical technique that allows the reader to absorb the content of a spread and grasp its content. What is observed with the eyes and other senses when looking at a spread? First impressions are crucial and become increasingly fluid with study, memorization, and familiarity with the meanings and attributions. A card's meanings will be modified and expanded by its location and neighbors, and readers must *see* this before they can apply their knowledge. Sight is the primary bridge between the cards on the table and the internal senses and knowledge of the reader. The eyes must be trained to scan the pattern of a spread in a useful way.

## PRELIMINARY EXERCISE

Shuffle a deck and spread out three cards. The first scan should be from left

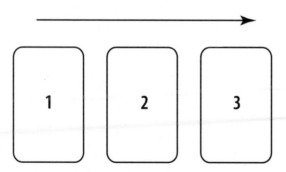

*Figure 20: Initial Scan of a Three-Card Spread*

---

19 Directional scanning is a term coined by the author to describe the visual observation technique for viewing a tarot spread.

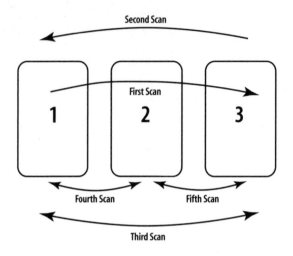

*Figure 21: A Complete Scan of a Three-Card Spread*

to right. Take in each card as it stands as an individual. Create a list of meanings for each card as is appropriate for that tarot deck.

Look for connections between neighbors: card 1 to 2; card 2 to 3. Scan the trio backward: card 3 to 2; card 2 to 1. Blend meanings; evaluate suits, numbers, elements, modes, and attributions. Take note of first impressions when the first visual sweeps of the spread are completed.

Allow your eyes to repeatedly scan back and forth between the different cards. Consider how the first and third cards surround the central card. Consider where the cards assist and flow, or if neighbors suppress or hinder—considerations of dignity. Finally, consider the combination as a whole—does it enjoy harmonious dignity, or do the cards debilitate each other?

Train your eyes and senses to absorb the combinations. Some readers approach cards from an intellectual standpoint; others use a sense-dependent technique that requires access to intuition, clairvoyance, gut instincts, and so on. Regardless of technique, the goal is to process the visual impressions of the spread to the mind; combine them silently with known divinatory meanings, attributions, and dignities; and finally to clearly communicate these assessments to the querent. It's perfectly acceptable to request moments of silence to absorb the cards before moving into verbalizing an interpretation.

## DIRECTIONAL SCANNING AND CROSS-TYPE SPREADS

This visual technique is necessary for all spreads, requiring an understanding of the inner pattern, the geometry, of the spread. The advantage of using cross-type spreads is that the movement of the eyes is the same, regardless of what type of cross spread is chosen and how many cards it contains. The Celtic Cross does not qualify as a cross-type spread, as the detached vertical row of four cards at the right hand of the central six-card cross hinders a smooth integration of its contents to the cross. The scanning requirements of a Celtic Cross spread make a synthesized interpretation needlessly difficult.

Always begin by scanning the horizontal axis, as this will give a feel for the querent's current concerns (even if this is you, the reader ). Then scan the vertical axis, as this shows how and where the querent's energies are being directed in his or her life. Assess the diagonal relationship between the cards at the axis points and how the card in the center modifies the relationship between the axis points. Proceed to evaluating the two hemispheres and quadrants, or in larger spreads, the diagonal axes.

Determine which axis or zone has the most clout by featuring trump cards, cards in locational or modal dignity, and dominant suits or numbers, and further note any hemisphere or quadrant with powerful cards. By approaching a spread in this manner, the thematic material being conveyed by the cards in the spread is apparent, revealed by placement and dignity. After thematic motifs are identified, add further detail to the interpretation by examining the relationships of the neighboring cards. A trump card on any point of the Cosmic Axis is a red flag, and its status in elemental, modal, zodiacal, locational, and numeric dignity is critical.

Figure 22 on pages 126–127 shows directional scanning patterns for various spread arrangements.

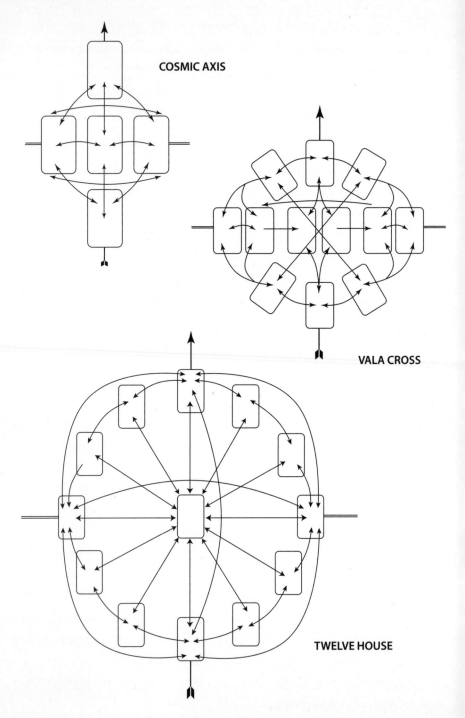

*Figure 22: Directional Scanning Patterns for Various Spread Arrangements*

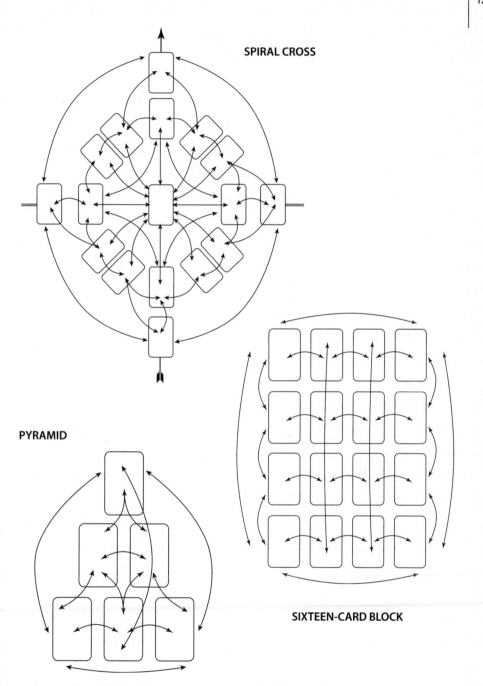

*Figure 22: Directional Scanning Patterns, continued*

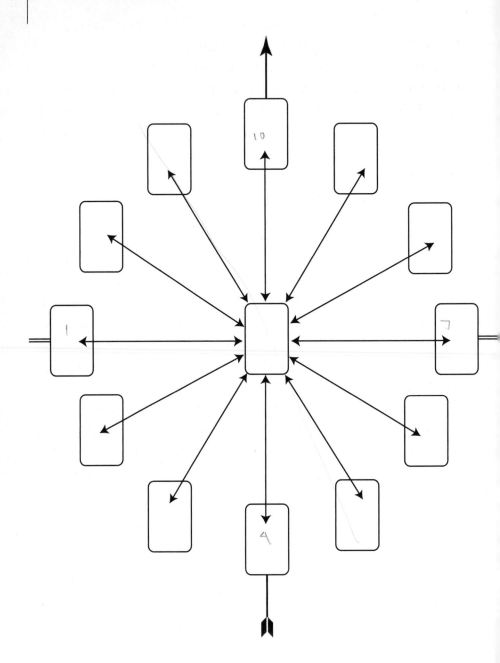

*Figure 23: House Polarity Scanning Pattern—Any Twelve-House Spread*

In any of the Twelve-House spreads, move the eye between the opposite houses: first house to seventh, second to eighth, and so on.

Although it may seem sufficient to move sequentially from first to second to third house, and so on, houses are activated through polar relationships and through the content of their modal cross. For instance, if there were trump cards in both the fifth and eleventh houses, that axis would gain priority in the reading. It would be useful to refer to the cards placed in the second/eighth houses as well, as those houses complete the fixed-mode cross.

By spreading the cards for a Twelve-House layout in a spiral format, the triple-cross pattern becomes distinctly integrated through card order and emphasizes the relationship of the three quaternities within the wheel. The final "cover" cards that may be used in any Twelve-House spread amplify the Cosmic Axis and aid in defining the core issues of the querent's life.

Dignity details that should consistently be noted are predominant numbers (sets or sequences), suits (elements and modes), zodiacal and planetary attributions, as well as trump cards that have lordship or affinity by sign, element, mode, number, or planet over the court and pip cards. These details animate the overall thematic material in the reading.

In a Twelve-House spread, the houses have a further triangular relationship, as shown in figure 24 on page 130. The elemental relationships of the signs (triplicities) form four interlocking triangles in a Twelve-House spread. The dignity between the cards in these triangles will show the ease or difficulty in the relevant areas of life. These elemental house relationships are as follows:

**First, fifth, ninth houses—fire:** the luckiest triad; individual expression and aspiration

**Second, sixth, tenth houses—earth:** the triad of work and effort, practical matters

**Third, seventh, eleventh houses—air:** the triad of relationships and communication

**Fourth, eighth, twelfth houses—water:** the most difficult triad; family and karma

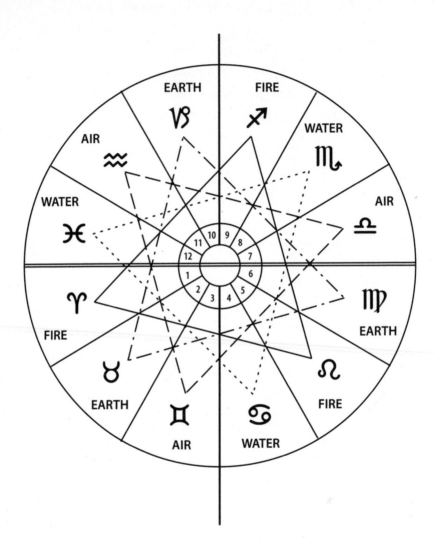

*Figure 24: Elemental Triplicities of Any Twelve-House Spread*

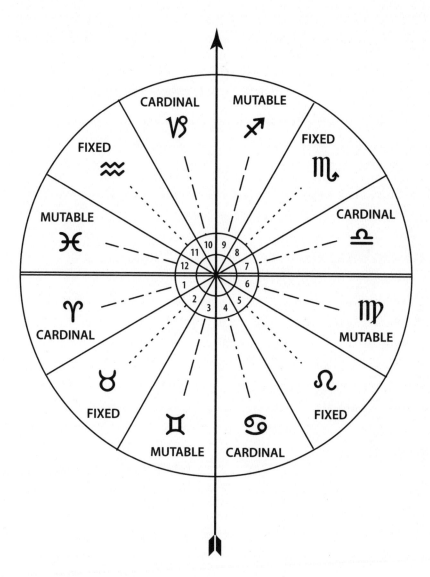

*Figure 25: Modal Quaternities of Any Twelve-House Spread*

Similarly, three interlocking crosses are created by the houses related by modality, as shown in figure 25 on page 131. These modal quaternities are:

**First, fourth, seventh, tenth houses—The Cosmic Axis:** cardinal signs or *angular* houses; relating to people and environments.

**Second, fifth, eighth, eleventh houses—fixed axis:** the *succeedent* houses; the basis of exchange in relationships with individuals and groups.

**Third, sixth, ninth, twelfth houses—mutable axis:** the *cadent* houses; the fruits of relationships and exchanges.

The three modal crosses should receive special attention, as these areas are integrated by meaning through the quadrants and hemispheres. Read the quaternities as you would read the Cosmic Axis—vertically, horizontally, and diagonally, back and forth, so that you can see how the cards are sharing their energies, attributions, and meanings with each other.

While the development of tarot spreads is expanding rapidly, cross-based spreads (excluding the Celtic Cross) should be a stock-in-trade for readers. From the simple five-card Cosmic Axis spread to the more elaborate Twelve-House spreads, there is a quality of elegance and consistent accuracy, broad application, and internal symmetry.

Pyramidal, or perhaps ziggurat, spreads flow from the bottom to the top. Visually, the two sides merge at the top; the two cards at either end of the bottom row coalesce at the center top card. The scanning technique is similar to that of a cross—the eyes flow along the bottom, then the edges, to the top, and finally sweep back down through the center to the bottom. In a spread with well-dignified cards, this scan will flow. In a spread with ill-dignified cards, the eyes will stumble and struggle to move along the sides to the top. If the card at the center of the bottom row conflicts with the top card, the querent should assess the appropriateness and timing of his or her goal. If the center bottom and top share good dignity, the querent's goals are within reach.

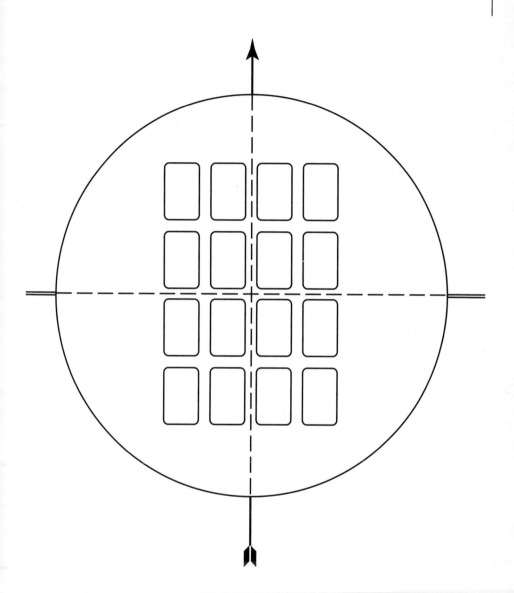

*Figure 26: Circling the Square into Quadrants and Hemispheres*

Nine-card square and sixteen-card block spreads require both horizontal and vertical scanning. Depending on how the cards are spread, the eye must move through the horizontal rows forward and backward and up and down through each vertical row. A block spread that has four rows of four cards each can be divided into quadrants and hemispheres—effectively circling the square through the imagination (see figure 26, page 133. The meanings of the quadrants and hemispheres can be superimposed on the position meanings.

Examine spreads for their shape and internal organization. Although positions may have specific meanings, the cards themselves will suggest their own meanings through placement and dignities. One may debate the usefulness of position meanings in general for this reason, as well as a tendency toward excessive reliance upon them in card interpretations. The tarotist with a fluent understanding of dignities won't need position meanings to derive an interpretation. The shape of a spread and the order of card placement in and of themselves define the meanings of the cards in their location.

## SYNTHESIS

Ultimately, the various analytical methods of interpretation—attributions and correspondences—are only useful to the extent that the reader can harvest them while scanning in order to verbalize their meaning to the client. For example, if the reader says to the client, *"You have the Empress (Venus) in good dignity, but she's hindered by the Nine of Swords (Mars in Gemini) in a detrimental location,"* the client will be bewildered. The dignities of the attributions must be conveyed in a meaningful way. The above example may be more usefully interpreted as, *"You have specific desires for the future, but scattered attention and fruitless quarrels hinder the attainment of these goals. There is a need to finish old business so that it ceases to be a distraction, and for more effective communication with people in situations that repeatedly provoke anger and frustration."*

Dignities, attributions, and correspondences are useful only if they add depth and breadth to interpretive skills and don't bog down interpretations—the desired result of a reading—with technical jargon. *Dignities and attributions are the goal of directional scanning and a foundation for spread evaluation.* These techniques are a reader's tools for gaining an interpretation that serves a client, not the end-product given to the client.

Many excellent tarot books offer detailed instructions for interpreting the symbolism rendered on the seventy-eight cards. The artistic attributions of repeated symbols and colors provide visual clues for interconnections between cards, and are arguably the primary device for tarot interpretation. Familiarity with the card images is mandatory. Combining the visual stimuli with the occult and cartomantic attributions is a sure path to magnifying the power and accuracy of the tarot as a divinatory tool.

Regardless of the attribution system chosen by the reader, the attributions must be memorized in order to harvest the dignities. Some tarot decks include attributions either in the renderings or along with the card name at the top or bottom. One benefit of memorizing attributions is that decks with unillustrated pip cards will be easier to use. The meanings of the elements, modes, numbers, zodiac signs, and planets are the foundation for understanding the of dignity in a tarot spread. The greater the facility for understanding these facets of dignity, the easier the reader will find interpreting the cards for him- or herself and others.

Nonetheless, dignity is a matter of great subtlety. The reader must determine which dignity factor gives the most weight to a particular card combination. Each spread layout will have dignity factors that are pertinent to the interpretation, but the combination of outstanding dignity features will be different for each reading. In some readings, the astrologically derived dignities will lend coherence to the thematic material; in other readings, the numeric dignities function as the predominant theme. Furthermore, one may find that certain dignity features are compelling during the first scan, while other connections are revealed by further observation. This may be equated with seeing the apparent surface (the most obvious factors), but eventually uncovering the deeper issues at work that are obscured by the surface façade. In this respect dignities really pull their weight in tarot reading and allow an incredibly deep and incisive interpretation that is, ultimately, of service to the client.

# CHAPTER 12

# DEMONSTRATIONS

T he art of tarot interpretation is composed of understanding how card combinations work together; blending meanings of neighboring cards through an assessment of dignity; and establishing the most important cards, card zones, or axis in a spread. Viewing a spread as a *whole* allows the reader to elucidate the dominant theme of a reading. The demonstrations offered in this chapter are intended to show how themes are found through dignities and combinations. Each spread is prefaced with an overview of the attributions and internal spread patterns, and the following interpretation shows how the dignities contribute an analytical foundation for understanding the spread.

From the standpoint of cohesive, holistic analysis, the cards should be spread into the selected layout (excepting the final cover cards) before verbalizing the interpretation so that the first impressions of the layout and initial thematic material indicated by the dignities can be identified. The reader can return to the card-by-card verbal interpretation for additional details. The directional scanning technique is employed to evaluate the card dignities. The reader is invited to reproduce these spreads with a tarot deck to enhance the learning process.

# DEMONSTRATION 1: COSMIC AXIS SPREAD

## The Cards in This Spread

**Card 1**—*Self,* Eight of Swords: (Jupiter/Gemini), air, mutable

**Card 2**—*Current Conditions/Moderator,* Five of Swords: (Venus/Aquarius), air, fixed

**Card 3**—*The Other, Interactions,* XX Judgment: planetary trump (Saturn), fire

**Card 4**—*Origins and Roots,* III Empress: planetary trump(Venus)

**Card 5**—*Outcomes,* Ace of Wands: elemental fire

## Overview of Dignities

**Elemental, Modal, Zodiacal, and Planetary Dignities**: Double air (cards 1 and 2) with fire (card 5). A pair of planetary trumps (Venus and Saturn). Judgment (Saturn) is the ruler of Aquarius (Five of Swords). Two modes are shown: mutable Eight of Swords and the fixed Five of Swords. The Five of Swords and the Empress share a Venus attribution; the Judgment and the Ace of Wands share a fire attribution.

**Missing**: No court cards, no cups, no pentacles, no cardinal.

**Numeric:** The vertical axis cards are all odd numbers (yang), while the cards on the horizontal axis points are even (yin). A subtle sequence exists in the Ace (1), Judgment (2), and the Empress (3).

**Locational Dignity:** Empress in the fourth house or IC position (the mother is in the home, so to speak); Judgment in the Descendant position (Saturn is exalted in the seventh house).

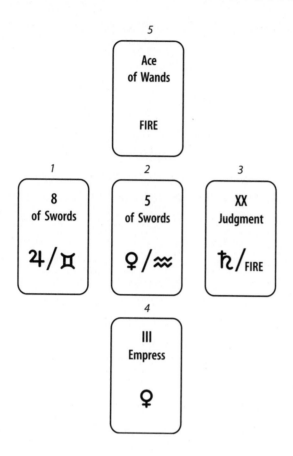

*Figure 27: The Empress Creates a New Life*

## Interpretation

The Eight and Five of Swords work as an opening pair. They indicate sorrow, failure, and anxiety; a sense of dread, entrapment. The querent's worries and fears exist in the present (Five of Swords in the center), and the regression from an Eight to a Five intimates that past judgments have led to current chaos or losses.

The Five of Swords/Judgment pair shows that the client's troubles are leading to a jarring encounter with awareness. This is a karmic test (Saturn) and probably a very hard pill to swallow. Saturn rules the Aquarian component of the Five of Swords, and Venus and Saturn are friends. Practicality, common sense, and hard work are required. A task faces the client: to come to terms with past failures and do what it takes to move forward, to create a stable foundation (Saturn) from the remnants of a very unstable environment (Five of Swords).

Judgment, in this instance, is tied to the external social factors of Aquarius. Although the client may have worked hard in the past (the number 8 = the sum of efforts, a judgment number), her past creations, skills, and results have not reached her intended audience (the airy Gemini/Aquarius factor). Perhaps the failure of communication is tied to a component of fear of awareness or fear of exposure, as the Eight of Swords implies isolation (further emphasized by the phobic Saturn at the opposite axis). There are no water cards to aid with emotional flow or earth cards to aid with practical efforts or accessible resources. Saturn exalts in the seventh house, so it's portending a near-future event of critical import. Reorganization and reprioritization are at hand, necessitated by the conscious awareness of false desires or useless goals (Five of Swords).

The Empress occupies the base of the reading—by locational dignity, an excellent placement. She, too, is tied to the Five of Swords by attribution (double Venus factor). The home and inner self are the primary targets of evaluation and reorganization (Saturn). The client's core values are poised at a crucial turning point. But the Empress is blocked on all fronts: the number 3 can't blend with either the number 8 (at the left diagonal) or 20 (at the right diagonal). The central 5, like Empress's 3, is a prime number. This Empress is frustrated—her abundant gifts, her love, and her joys, are not being shared. Her highest ideals have collapsed, as shown by the Five of Swords. The normally fruitful nature of Venus is now compelled to work within the restrictive terms of Judgment and is forced to compare her values to those of the collective community (Five of Swords = Aquarius). She has only herself and her own gifts and talents upon which to rely (Eight of Swords).

So the Empress at the base of this spread must retreat (Five of Swords) in order to discern how to consolidate, regroup, and undo the chaotic circumstances of the present. The Ace of Wands, the card of elemental fire, tops the spread and gleans two meanings from the prior cards: the Empress must gather the pieces (Five of Swords) to magically reassemble them into a new form of life (Ace/fire), and the son (Ace) will usurp the role of the father (Saturn) as old foundations give way to new.

The hopeful factor in the reading is the planetary attributions of the horizontal axis: Jupiter and Saturn are at opposite points, bookending Venus between them. Growth and contraction are having a direct influence on the desires and values of the client. This implies a controlled, mature focus on primal ambitions and survival (Ace of Wands). The Ace encompasses the meanings of a bonfire for signals, or the rising Sun (growing awareness), so the Empress is being instructed to send signals to the world, to make fire magic with the parts and pieces she has at hand, with the understanding that this outreach will offer new opportunities. There is an underlying theme that neglected or forgotten efforts from the past (Eight of Swords/Empress), now lying dormant, may be coming to light (Ace) from sources in the outer world (Saturn).

To complete the analysis, a final cover card is drawn for the center position—it's the World (XXI). This is a good omen for several reasons. The World-Judgment combination is always quite powerful and signals a critical decision or turning point that is full of fate. There are dramatic karmic overtones, and the forces of time and space, cause and effect, are at full potency. The Empress's number 3 is a denominator of 21, so the Empress can find the key (21 divided by 3 = 7) to making changes in her life through prayer, patience, and faith, attributes of the number seven.

The World, as a card of Earth and spirit, partakes of the primal powers of creation and development. Saturn provides the form, Venus supplies the egg, the Ace the sperm, and the World a nurturing womb for the seed to develop. The burst of animating force provided by the Ace of Wands shows the future outcome is toward a transformed incarnation, leaving the old shell of broken values and goals (Five of Swords) in the past.

# DEMONSTRATION 2: THE VALA CROSS

This example (figure 28 on page 143) focuses on court cards. To summarize the functions of the trumps, court cards, and pip cards:

**The Major Arcana** (twenty-two trump cards) express the dominant forces at work, inexorable archetypal patterns that arrange and compel the courts and pips into enacting mythic models.

**The Court Cards** (sixteen cards, Page through King) act on/act out the imperatives of the trumps and are further qualified in motivations and environment by neighboring pips.

**The Pip Cards** (forty cards, Ace through Ten) show the interplay of actions and conditions as informed by the trumps and courts.

## The Cards in This Spread

Card 1—**King of Swords:** (Taurus/Gemini), mutable air, fire status

Card 2—**Seven of Swords:** (Moon/Aquarius), fixed air

Card 3—**Justice:** (Libra), cardinal air, zodiacal trump

Card 4—**Wheel:** (Jupiter), planetary trump

Card 5—**King of Cups:** (Aquarius/Pisces), mutable water, fire status

Card 6—**Two of Cups:** (Venus/Cancer), cardinal water

Card 7—**Four of Wands:** (Venus/Aries), cardinal fire

Card 8—**Chariot:** (Cancer), cardinal water, zodiacal trump

Card 9—**Knight of Swords:** (Capricorn/Aquarius), fixed air, air status (double element court card)

Card 10—**Ten of Pentacles:** (Mercury/Virgo), mutable earth

Card 11—**Nine of Pentacles:** (Venus/Virgo), mutable earth

Card 12—**Ace of Swords:** elemental air

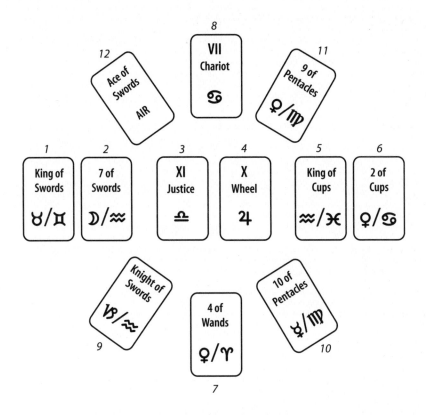

*Figure 28: Kings at the Axis Points*

## Overview of Dignities

- A pair of Kings (one air, one water, both mutable) occupy opposite ends of the horizontal axis.
- A pair of trumps are in the center (Libra—cardinal air; Jupiter).
- The Nine and Ten of Pentacles (mutable earth) in the western hemisphere are in contrast to
- The Knight and Ace of Swords (fixed, air) in the eastern hemisphere.
- The Kings are paired with a pip card of the same suit at their respective axis points.

- The two central trumps are capped with a zodiacal trump (Cancer) at the Midheaven position, and both zodiacal trumps are of cardinal modality.
- A pair of Sevens (Seven of Swords plus the Chariot).
- Three Venus pip cards (Four of Wands, Two of Cups, Nine of Pentacles).
- A diagonal axis features a set of several number 1s: Ace of Swords, the Wheel, and Ten of Pentacles (in the tenth card position), along with a double 1 in the Justice card (eleventh trump).
- The eastern hemisphere is dominated by air.
- The western hemisphere is balanced between water and earth.
- Cardinal fire occupies the IC.
- Cardinal water occupies the MC.
- The secondary axis is a repeated pattern of air-earth on these axis points.

## Interpretation

The Kings in this reading (and court cards in general) represent the roles, functions, and characteristics of their suit's elements as expressed by their assigned zodiacal cusps. They may be considered as specific individuals, groups, social roles, or as personal characteristics that are important to the querent as traits to develop or traits that others may display in the environment.

The King of Swords lies on the Ascendant, thus representing the querent. At the opposite point lies the King of Cups at the Descendant, so he represents the other. The King of Swords is the master of ideas and thoughtful purpose, but he looks perplexed and uncertain in proximity to the Seven of Swords, as though he has sent his messengers to wing but is unsure of a response. Legal matters and political thoughts permeate his situation, as he's near the elementally related Justice card (airy Libra). Action should be taken, but timing is critical. The Wheel signals swift, energetic changes and rearrangements being initiated within the environment (Jupiter with cardinal Libra).

Management and organization are crucial, but external forces of social organizations are applying pressure to act, to change, to grow with the times.

The opposite King of Cups stands in fair dignity as neighboring Jupiter rules Pisces, his sign. This King also enjoys the company of the Two of Cups. Meetings with good news are in store, perhaps in two separate endeavors (notice several sets of pairs in this reading; in addition, the two Kings are of the mutable, or twin, signs). The combinations in this spread emphasize multiplicity and reaching beyond normal boundaries.

Messages arriving at the home are strongly indicated by the combination of the Four of Wands and Ten of Pentacles in the lower hemisphere. The Knight of Swords travels to the home. The Ten of Pentacles is the *summum bonum*, the Great Work; both pips imply agreements and balance on different fronts. The Four of Wands suggests creative, personal benefits (Venus), perhaps invitations to parties and celebrations, assistance from friends. The Ten of Pentacles brings professional benefits and stability to the second quadrant of personal development, and mutually lucrative opportunities are shown in the western hemisphere through the association of the King and Two of Cups with the Nine and Ten of Pentacles.

Immediate action and initiative are shown with the Chariot at the Midheaven axis, with good news arriving from a distant location (Jupiter, which exalts in Cancer). Mail and phone contacts are in store with the airy qualities of the Knight and Ace of Swords; proposals should be considered for pros and cons (Ace). The Seven of Swords shows a need to clarify goals and objectives. The pair of Sevens both have lunar attributions that are problematic factors in this spread. The Knight of Swords rules the Seven of Swords (both Aquarian), thus indicating irritating confusions, delays, conflicting priorities, and uncertain timing. The querent may not have the luxury of time to make full investigations on potential offers, or decisions may be followed by uncomfortable periods of waiting.

The Chariot at the Midheaven shows the overall direction of the querent in the future. The commanding intellectual influences in the eastern (left) hemisphere that are reasonably comfortable with risk-taking are going to struggle with the water/earthy influence of the western (right) hemisphere that prefer comfortable guarantees. Indeed, the Chariot card embodies the struggle between intellect and emotions and the need to balance and harness these qualities for effective forward movement.

The diagonal axis with the Ace of Swords over Justice, the Wheel, and the Ten of Pentacles shows dramatic incentive or information on a particularly important subject. Agreements will be a key factor in transforming future efforts. The Chariot is exceptionally compulsive: the tricky juggling act between internalized components is challenged by the equally cardinal yet externalized Justice card (Libra). Justice requires emotional detachment to determine the benefits and values of offers and agreements—the King of Swords must be able to discern the extent of his time and resources quickly! Chance encounters and lightning swift exchanges of information will rattle the King's composure. The King can't always control his Knight either!

Still, the central trumps indicate a flow of sheer luck, as Jupiter exalts in Cancer (Wheel/Chariot) and can bring long-desired goals to pass on many levels, particularly in public, government, or organizational levels. New associations being built can be rendered particularly helpful (Four of Wands) if they involve shared enthusiasms.

So, although the King of Swords may be a bit jumbled, this spread gives, overall, beneficial indications because it lacks malefic influences (Mars or Saturn) by attribution. With the Moon, Venus, and Jupiter as the predominant planetary rulers, blessings arrive through personal connections, relatives, friends, and associates that share and promote ideologies or goals in common with the querent. People who think alike find each other and interact in a favorable manner. Kindness and courtesy are emphasized in future dealings, as Libra rules the graces, and peace-loving signs occupy the western (other-oriented) hemisphere: Cancer, Virgo, and Pisces.

As befits an exchange between court characters, the King of Swords would do well to appeal to the vanity and pleasure-loving nature of the King of Cups and infuse his business dealings with amenities. He would also do well to see past the flattery that may be offered by the King of Cups in order to seduce the King of Swords to his way of thinking. The three Venus cards in the spread (the Four of Wands, Two of Cups, and Nine of Pentacles) all appear in the western hemisphere, which suggests that things that the querent values are being offered to him by others, or may be gained through association.

All the factors supplied in the overview of dignities act as components for the interpretation. The dominant theme of this spread shows that negotiations are subject to the cause-and-effect mechanism. The capacity for swift analysis and decisive action (with imperviousness to seduction or appeals made to the desire nature) are the qualities most needed by the querent.

The trump cards that occupy the vertical axis make this the outstanding area of the spread, and they emphasize both origin and destination. The contrast of elements between the cards in the eastern and western hemispheres adds a cautionary note—that timing is an important factor in assessing the guaranteed options versus the more risky options. This hemispheric balance also implies that the offers from others (west) are more likely to be rooted in stable foundations (earth and water), whereas the projects initiated by the querent (east) are likely to be more risky.

## DEMONSTRATION 3: TWELVE-HOUSE SPREAD

### The Cards in This Spread

Position = House (first card is in the first house)—attributions are as follows:

Card 1—**King of Pentacles:** (Leo/Virgo cusp), mutable earth, fire status

Card 2—**King of Swords:** (Taurus/Gemini cusp), mutable air, fire status

Card 3—**Eight of Cups:** (Saturn/Pisces), mutable water

Card 4—**Seven of Cups:** (Venus/Scorpio), fixed water (Venus in detriment)

Card 5—**Ace of Wands:** elemental fire

Card 6—**Queen of Swords:** (Virgo/Libra cusp), cardinal air, water status

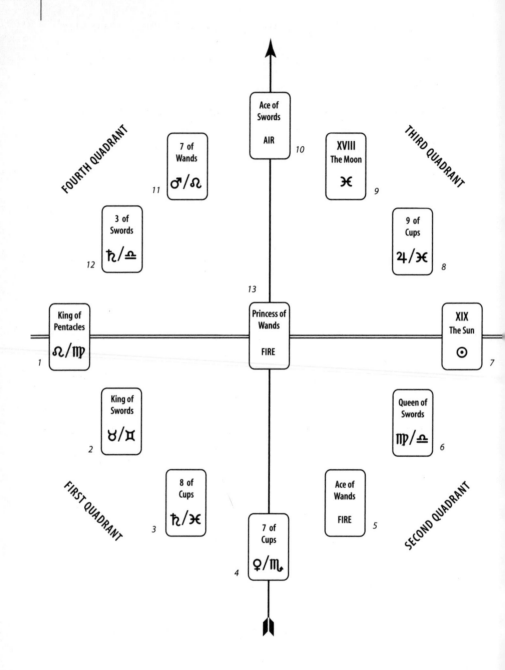

*Figure 29: Princess Reaches for the Sword*

**Card 7—XIX The Sun:** planetary trump (Sun)

**Card 8—Nine of Cups:** (Jupiter/Pisces), mutable water (Jupiter in rulership)

**Card 9—XVIII The Moon:** zodiacal trump (Pisces), mutable water

**Card 10—Ace of Swords:** elemental air

**Card 11—Seven of Wands:** (Mars/Leo), fixed fire

**Card 12—Three of Swords:** (Saturn/Libra), cardinal air (Saturn in exaltation)

**Card 13—Princess of Wands:** (central card), fire, Earth status

## Overview of Dignities

**Numeric/Cartomantic:** Pair of Aces, pair of Kings, pair of Sevens; Seven, Eight, Nine of Cups sequence; King, Queen of Swords sequence; Sun-Moon trump sequence; Moon (18 = 1 + 8 = 9) and Nine of Cups are a pair of Nines; pair of Saturn pip cards.

**Zodiacal/Planetary:** King of Pentacles and Queen of Swords own sequential decans (Leo, Virgo, Libra). Mutable water in third quadrant; the second and fourth quadrants feature fire-air balance. Three elemental cards (two Aces and Princess of Wands). Planetary pairs Sun and Moon, Venus and Mars, Jupiter and Saturn are represented.

**Locational:** XIX Sun is in fall in the seventh house. Queen of Swords in sixth = Virgo component is placed in natural house. Earth triplicity (second, sixth, and tenth houses) occupied by air sequence—King, Queen, and Ace of Swords. Fifth to eleventh axis is occupied by three fire cards (Ace, Princess, and Seven of Wands). A nine card (Moon) is in the ninth house.

## Analysis by Axis

### The Cosmic Axis

First house, King of Pentacles + (center, Princess of Wands) + seventh house, XIX Sun (mutable earth—elemental fire—the Sun): Querent in role of mastering stability, earthly matters. Partnerships are critical to success, but some struggles in achieving goals (Sun in fall in the seventh). Partners may not embody order, methodology as desired. King must use capacity for fiery inspiration (Princess + his Leo decan of rulership).

Fourth house, Seven of Cups + (center, Princess) + tenth house, Ace of Swords (fixed water—fire—air): This axis mixes three elements. Watery hopes and wishes are at the origin or base of the reading, emphasizing emotional contemplation and inner examination of goals of the King of Pentacles. Princess of Wands sparks action, ignition of deep desires; Ace of Swords represents knowledge flow—both in and out. Heightened awareness activates the dreamy nature of the Seven of Cups and a clear view of the pros and cons of new opportunities.

In the Cosmic Axis, the seventh and tenth houses have the most powerful cards, so partnerships, interactions, and future choices are critical. The querent's life path is at a tremendous crossroad of possibility and discovery.

### Second House/Eighth House Axis

King of Swords + (center, Princess) + Nine of Cups (mutable air—fire—mutable water): This is the axis of exchange and shows mutable cards on a fixed axis. The King's ability to distinguish, comprehend, and access are quite specific, but the results are general, diffused by the Pisces attribution. Joy comes from an alternate quarter—literally. The King's efforts may not get direct results.

### Third House/Ninth House Axis

Eight of Cups + (center, Princess) + XVIII the Moon (mutable water—fire—mutable water): This is the axis of communication, a mutable axis occupied by mutable cards that share a zodiacal attribution. Both cards are members of important sequences. Issues from the past, historic patterns and phases, the dead or disembodied spirits are all sources of communication. The Moon in the ninth house indicates access to the unconscious mind, a view of what is behind the veil. Blood and water and moon mysteries are the substance of the conceptual influence on the querent. The Moon in this location also indicates the travel of natural phenomena (during the reading, the tropical storm Lili was approaching from the south, bringing extremes of rain and wind). Querent becomes aware of tragedies at a distance, the world gone amok. The Princess must recognize these influences and interpret their meaning.

### Fifth House/Eleventh House Axis

Ace of Wands + (center, Princess) + Seven of Wands (fire—fire—fixed fire): This is the axis of expression and results. The three Wand cards are well dignified on this axis, and the Seven of Wands lends its fixed modality to a fixed axis. Two aspects of nascent fire, the Ace and Princess, signify powerful bursts of creativity, inspiration, and love. The Seven of Wands indicates that this may be too much to handle with ease—there is an overflow of pure hungry fire that can't easily be mastered. The Seven of Wands in the eleventh house combines two mystic numbers, 7 and 11. Delays are related to mystic timing; impediments and distractions are a test of mastery and skill in expression. Results will be gained, but at a high cost. This card's attribution of Mars/Leo completes the planetary pair with the Seven of Cups, Venus/Scorpio, and ties together the pair of Sevens. Periods of waiting must be infused with spiritual calm, in spite of pressure from extremes.

### Sixth House/Twelfth House Axis

Queen of Swords + (center, Princess) + Three of Swords (cardinal air—fire—cardinal air): This is the axis of dharma and karma. The Queen of Swords "owns" the Three of Swords, so it brings a slight improvement to the location of cardinal cards placed on a mutable axis. The Queen is the most skillful yet the loneliest of the Queens. She has learned to endure isolation, pain and anguish, and her private demons, yet in this location health problems are indicated—aches, pains, inner torment, and exhaustion.

This axis also reveals delays, anxieties, confusion, and a struggle to cope. Since the Queen possesses the third decan of Virgo, she has more mature coping skills and may draw upon hidden strengths. She can be effective in the face of pain and sorrow, shielding herself from the worst of it. She must make lemonade out of lemons here. In the Three of Swords, Saturn exalts in Libra, the sign of law, order, and authority. The Queen may have specific fears about unknown aspects of legal, health, or spiritual issues. Her anxiety is derived from her lack of control over authority figures, her inability to counter delays, or a perceived lack of leverage in agreements. This aspect of the querent's condition is likely well hidden beneath the surface façade of the King of Pentacles. Cardinal-mode cards on a mutable axis don't possess the means to call the shots—they have to wait and take things as they come.

## Analysis by Quadrants

### First Quadrant: Personal/Inner Area

[King of Pentacles] + King of Swords + Eight of Cups + [Seven of Cups]. This quadrant features a key pair and members of pairs and sequences in the spread. The attribution sequence is: mutable earth, mutable air, mutable water, fixed water. The inner life of the querent is defined by the sequence of Cup cards that is resolved in the eighth house (Nine of Cups). This watery numeric sequence occupies critical locations in the spread. The mystic Seven and capable Eight must result in the karmic Nine, enacted through the element of water. There is a need for flow, release, acceptance, and a capacity for both sorrow and joy. This quadrant reveals the challenges faced by the querent, the inner challenges (Seven, Eight) and the level of testing (Kings = mastery, the ability to transform and fertilize). The querent faces both the demands of mystic contemplation and acceptance and the need to catalyze authoritative judgment in the realms of earth (practical matters) and air (intellectual puzzles).

### Second Quadrant: Development/Inner Area

[Seven of Cups] + Ace of Wands + Queen of Swords + [XIX the Sun]. The attribution sequence is: fixed water—elemental fire—cardinal air—Sun. This is a powerful quadrant of the spread, with strong dignities occupying the fifth and sixth houses. The Ace of Wands in the fifth house is in excellent dignity, a card of birth in the house of birth and expression. This placement shows an explosion of inner fire, expression unhindered, the inspiration of the divine muse in the process of creation. The Queen of Swords is skillful at managing and organizing. She channels the fire, blending the fixed water of the Seven of Cups with the elemental fire of the Ace to her own advantage. She must work with extreme contrasts of energy. The Sun and the Ace of Wands surround the Queen and encompass her with powerful light. New working relationships and tasks are evolving; she must define her role, bring order to new sources of knowledge, and implement her skills. Intuition and intelligence are combined. Knowledge that is shared brings illumination, bright ideas, and triumphs. On the spiritual level, the Queen has the potential to illuminate her darkest fears and the choice to release them.

### Third Quadrant: Interpersonal/Outer Area

[XIX the Sun] + Nine of Cups +XVIII the Moon + [Ace of Swords]. The attribution sequence is: Sun—mutable water—mutable water—elemental air. The third and fourth quadrants impact the lower hemisphere and show the issues that the inner self must contend with and the potential for exchange of influence between the inner and outer hemispheres. The third quadrant has specific influence on the first quadrant. The Sun and the Nine of Cups show a benevolent source of influence—triumphs through the influence of others, a growing reputation, and welcome assistance given to the querent. Jupiter is in rulership in Pisces (Nine of Cups) and extends his benefic energies by placement in a watery house. The Sun illuminates the mystic and spiritual when it neighbors watery cards and orients the Nine of Cups toward lasting results in the flow of time. Wisdom is manifest with this combination. The Nine of Cups and the Moon share the zodiacal attribution of Pisces. Although the Moon is a difficult card, it receives good dignity next to the Nine because of the expansive strength of Jupiter. However, this is the oceanic Jupiter, and it evokes mystical, magical, and invisible sources, the flow of both light and darkness. The Sun and the Moon are the light of day and the light of night, and both represent powerful external influences on the querent, who must balance extremes of nature and extreme personalities in their environment. Both blessings and curses are at work, and if the veil is torn from hidden matters, it will be a mixed blessing, as shown by the Ace of Swords. All new information and awareness must be evaluated for light/dark, open and hidden motives. The Moon brings the power of the eclipse and the ebb and flow of lunar cycles, while the Sun is steady yet potentially overpowering.

### Fourth Quadrant: Results/Outer Area

[Ace of Swords] + Seven of Wands + Three of Swords + [King of Pentacles]. The attribution sequence is: elemental air—fixed fire—cardinal air—mutable earth. This is the most predictive quadrant, showing the outcome of activity in the first three quadrants, and it contains the most difficult cards in the spread. These cards show a struggle in coping with the extreme energies of the third quadrant. The eleventh- and twelfth-house cards are attributed to the two malefics, Mars and Saturn. These cards complete the construction of planetary pairs in this spread—Venus and Mars, Jupiter and Saturn, the Sun and Moon. Although the third quadrant assures benefits through association, the fourth quadrant shows unavoidable difficulties along the path to success.

The only planet omitted from these sets is Mercury. Mercury is embodied in the King of Pentacles/Queen of Swords pair (sharing a Virgo component). The querent must combine the talents of these two court cards to manage the extremes of all three major planetary pairs shown in this spread. The Seven of Wands shows courageous struggles, good intentions, difficult physical challenges, and striving to achieve against the odds. In the eleventh house, some goals will be reached, while others elude the querent's reach or slip through the cracks. The Three of Swords in the twelfth house is tough, and suggests anxieties, aches and pains, losses, and uncontrollable side effects. There is frustration because of indecision, bad timing, or inconvenient delays. The cards in the mutable axis (third, sixth, ninth, and twelfth houses) are the Eight of Cups, Queen of Swords, the Moon, and the Three of Swords—all difficult cards at cross-purposes with their locations, except for the Queen of Swords. The perceptual abilities of the Queen (in the sixth) must be merged with the earth mastery of the King of Pentacles (in the first)—this is the key to results in this spread. The second and fourth quadrants show fire-air combinations attempting to cope with the Seven, Eight, Nine of Cups water sequence.

## Thematic Conclusion

The cards in this spread are distinctly intertwined. The watery sequence underscores the plotline of a difficult stage of development—the Seven and Eight lead to the karmic Nine. A trio of elementals (two Aces and a Princess) and the Sun/Moon present the chief challenges located in the second and third quadrants and indicate both internal and external sources of turbulence. Matters reach extremes, and the challenge is to adapt to the moment without losing sight of long-term goals—a task that mandates the merger of the King of Pentacles and the Queen of Swords.

The King, Queen, and Ace of Swords occupy the earth triplicity houses in this spread (figure 30 on page 156). Air (thought) must penetrate matter (earth) to be effective. This triplicity unites the Queen and King to give birth to the Ace. The Ace is the prize of battle, a symbol of the power of war, conflict, and conquest. The liberty of the Princess of Wands (earth status) at the center shows that the airy cards in the earthy triplicity feed the pure flame of her being.

The themes of this spread are coping with extremes and being tested to the limits of endurance. There is a perilous path to the ultimate goal. The querent can't lose sight of the prize, regardless of distractions and interruptions, and must remain faithful in times of darkness and uncertainty. This is a time of powerful fate for the querent (the Sun/the Moon), characterized by battles for inner wholeness—the struggle to unify the Queen of Swords with the King of Pentacles. The ultimate union is at hand, enacted through choices and actions. No mistakes may be made (pair of Kings). The pure faith and spirit of the Princess is contained in a frail, earthly body. The events at hand for the querent may exceed the limits of the container.

The Princess of Wands interpolates and moderates the axes of the spread, but as the thirteenth card she is also the result. It's her light that

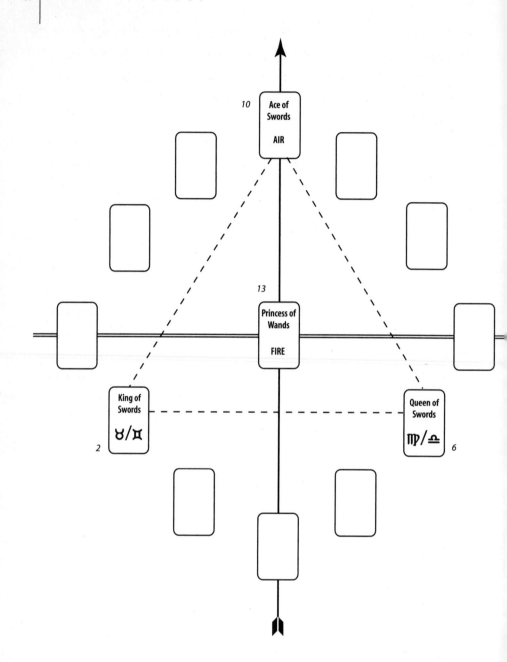

*Figure 30: Earth Triplicity*

guides the querent to achieving the Ace of Swords at the apex of the spread. This princess is the essence of the chemistry of combustion, and she rules the galactic quadrant of the North Pole, which contains the constellation of Draco, the dragon, and Polaris, the North Star. The Ace over her head is like the North Star, so the Princess must use her inner light and capacity for unimpeded combustion to navigate toward her goal. She must embody "irrational enthusiasm,"[20] consuming both light and darkness, and apply her sense of daring and sheer force of character to gain her ends. Above all, she must believe in herself with "omnivorous passion."[21] The Princess is tied to her natural axis (fifth-eleventh) by suit, so she has an avenue of expression for her element. She thrills to the challenges presented—all of it becomes fuel for her, everything put to use. She is reckless, yet oriented by the intellectual brilliance of the cards in the earth triplicity. The princess has all the power she needs, but the weapon remains just beyond her grasp. In reaching for her prize of conquest, she must be smart yet willing to risk it all—logic feeds her intuition. She must make a daring leap to attain the Sword. The goals of the spread are within reach, yet the riskiest moment lies ahead of the querent.

20 Aleister Crowley, *The Book of Thoth* (New York: U.S. Games Systems, 1969), 155.
21 Ibid, 155.

# DEMONSTRATION 4: THE ZODIAC SPIRAL SPREAD

## The Cards in This Spread

Card 1, center—X Wheel of Fortune: (Jupiter)

*Cosmic Axis:*

Card 2, first house—Ace of Pentacles: (earth)

Card 3, fourth house—Six of Cups: (Sun/Scorpio) mutable water

Card 4, seventh house—Two of Wands: (Mars/Aries) cardinal fire

Card 5, tenth house—Eight of Swords: (Jupiter/Gemini) mutable air

*Fixed Axis:*

Card 6, second house—Knight of Cups: (Libra/Scorpio) fixed water

Card 7, fifth house—Nine of Swords: (Mars/Gemini) mutable air

Card 8, eighth house—King of Wands: (Scorpio/Sagittarius) mutable fire

Card 9, eleventh house—King of Swords: (Taurus/Gemini) mutable air

*Mutable Axis:*

Card 10, third house—Five of Swords: (Venus/Aquarius) fixed air

Card 11, sixth house—Two of Pentacles: (Jupiter/Capricorn) cardinal earth

Card 12, ninth house—Five of Pentacles: (Mercury/Taurus) fixed earth

Card 13, twelfth house—XIV Temperance: (Sagittarius) mutable fire

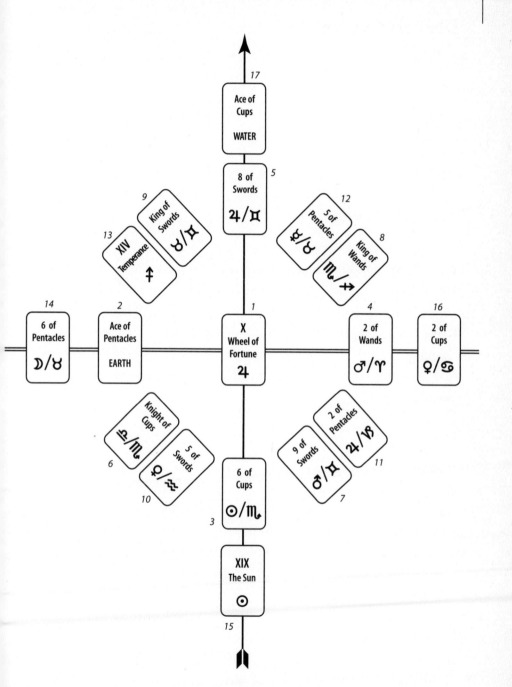

*Figure 31: The Wheel at the Crossroads*

### Cosmic Axis Cover Cards

**Card 14,** first house—Six of Pentacles: (Moon/Taurus) fixed earth

**Card 15,** fourth house—XIX The Sun: (Sun)

**Card 16,** seventh house—Two of Cups: (Venus/Cancer) cardinal water

**Card 17,** tenth house—Ace of Cups: water

## Overview of Dignities

A set of number 1s: Sun, Ace of Cups, Ace of Pentacles, Wheel of Fortune. Three 2s: a pair of Kings, a pair of Sixes, a pair of Fives. Ace in the first house. MC/IC axis is a set of 1s (Ace, Wheel, Sun). Fifth-eleventh axis—King and Nine of Swords (both Gemini). Water Triplicity—fourth house with Six of Cups (Sun/Scorpio) and the Sun; eighth house with King of Wands (Sagittarius); and twelfth house with Temperance (Sagittarius)—fiery cards in watery houses. Wheel of Fortune in center of the spread, the first card position.

## Brief Analysis

With the number 1 on three axis points and in the center, the querent is in a phase of multiple beginnings. However, the partnership area is heavily tenanted with 2s, an indication of extreme turmoil and heightened activity connected with people in the querent's life. The pair of Fives occupies the third-ninth axis of communications, another sign that exchanges with others are fraught with tensions, difficulties, and delays. The Eight of Swords in the tenth house echoes this theme of gridlock and confusion.

Nevertheless, some areas of the spread show positive flow and the potential for good results. The Knight of Cups and the King of Wands on the second-eighth axis share contiguous decans (Libra, Scorpio, and Sagittarius), so the Knight in the second house is growing toward the King in the eighth. The desired exchanges require steady effort as well as sensitivity about the needs of others. Good cards that emphasize solar qualities and contentment occupy the base of the reading (fourth house) but are bookended by the Five and Nine of Swords. Although the home is secure, there are definite indications of unfortunate conditions in the daily environment, particularly around friends (fifth).

The eleventh and twelfth houses are occupied by good cards. The King of Swords "owns" the Nine of Swords in the opposite axis—troubles are mitigated by good advice and professional assistance. The Temperance card (which features an angel in its symbolism) implies that hidden or unseen forces are working benevolently on behalf of the querent, and unexpected good luck or sudden breakthroughs are possible.

The strongest axis of this spread is the Midheaven/Nadir axis. There is a set of 1s: XIX the Sun card, which is paired with a Sun pip card (Six of Cups—Sun/Scorpio); X the Wheel (Jupiter), paired with a Jupiter pip card in the Eight of Swords; and the Ace of Cups. Although the Eight of Swords does imply waiting and frustration, the vigorous influence of the Sun and Jupiter along this axis signals that delays might be advantageous to the querent.

The Ascendant/Descendant axis is also distinctive. The Ace and Six of Pentacles, two earthy cards, occupy the Ascendant. The querent is experiencing fortunate gains and benefits from generosity. The Twos on the opposite axis are cardinal cards in a cardinal house. This pair of Twos is attributed to the planetary pair Venus and Mars—an appropriate pair for the house of partnerships. This suggests partnerships beginning on different levels—in emotional affinities and in fledgling opportunities for ambition. Because the cluster of 2s represents significant flux with others, it's appropriate to consider the origin of these individuals.

The Two of Cups provides the clues. It relates to the Six of Cups in the fourth house, and the Ace of Cups in the tenth house. The Six of Cups (surrounded by fretful swords) shows that contact is being reestablished with dear friends from the past mired in difficult problems. The Sun card beneath the Six of Cups shows that friends seek warmth and illumination from the querent—perhaps a chance to retrieve some of the happiness of their former relationship. The Ace of Cups in the tenth indicates a new friend, someone with whom the querent makes contact out in the world. Since the Eight of Swords slows the Ace of Cups with delays and frustrations, this meeting may come about by waiting in line for service, or while seeking aid for a similar problem.

This new relationship is the source of a powerful (if unexpected) attraction. The King of Swords and the Temperance card suggest that "opposites attract" (Gemini/Sagittarius cards = opposite signs). The Six of Cups in the fourth house also shows that the querent may be open to romance, even if not consciously admitting it, and may be caught up in critical adjustments with the Wheel in the center of the spread. The Wheel casts its influence around the entire spread but is an important source of impetus for the pair of Aces. The Ace of Pentacles in the first house enjoys locational dignity and shows the querent is building new foundations in his life path. But the Ace of Cups in the tenth shows an unexpected encounter with a potential new lover. Since the Nine of Swords appears in the fifth house of love and is a card of embarrassment, the querent would be well advised to dress well in all circumstances and be prepared for anything when leaving home.

Although the spread answered questions that the querent had about his career opportunities and was correct in the assessment of reestablishing old friendships, the querent didn't expect opportunities for a new romance at the time of the reading. But the Wheel often brings changes beyond a querent's expectations, and this card's location at the center of the spread and its participation in a sequence along the MC/IC axis creates an incredibly pervasive influence on the entire spread.

· · ·

As shown in the demonstrations, dignities and attributions can be used in both simple and complex ways to extract meaning from a spread. The astrologically derived dignities may take years to master, but are well worth the effort for the information they provide about interconnections between the cards and spread positions.

Tarot cards have layers of meanings; likewise there are multiple layers of dignity techniques for clarifying the focus of a card's divinatory meaning. For those who are dedicated, the study of new techniques and possibilities for usage will continue to increase the breadth and depth of interpretive skills. This study is a worthy goal of a lifetime; even after all my years as a tarotist, I still discover new facets of the cards in almost every reading.

The contemporary understanding and usage of attribution systems is in a state of flux. Older and newer systems coexist and all have their good points. The established Golden Dawn system, now over one hundred years old, may be subjected to tinkering as new planets are discovered and occult study progresses. As can be seen with the mythologies and metaphysical philosophies handed down from antiquity, occult systems are prone to mutations, adjusted applications, mergers, and redefinition through the lens of cultural bias. Systems are neither sacred nor immutable, although the really old ones (like elemental relationships and astrological dignities) do seem to retain their authority. For this reason, the tarotist is advised to embrace the Saturnian demands of memorization and dedicated study, while also adhering to the Jovian principles of accepting change and alternative concepts with good humor. I leave you with this adjuration from Henry Cornelius Agrippa:

> Moreover whatsoever thou operatest, do it with an earnest affection and hearty desire; that the goodness of the heavens and heavenly bodies may favour thee, whose favour, that thou mayest more easily obtain, the fitness of the place, time, profession, custom, diet, habit, exercise and name also do wonderfully conduce: for by these the power of nature is not only changed, but also overcome.[22]

---

22 Henry Cornelius Agrippa, "Of certain religious observations, ceremonies, and rites of perfumings, unctions, and such like," in *Three Books of Occult Philosophy* (St. Paul, MN: Llewellyn, 2000), 672.

# APPENDICES

# GOLDEN DAWN CARD ATTRIBUTIONS

## ATTRIBUTIONS FOR THE MAJOR ARCANA

| Card | Attribution | Element | Mode |
|------|-------------|---------|------|
| 0 Fool | *Uranus** | **Air**** | |
| I Magician | Mercury | | |
| II High Priestess | Moon | | |
| III Empress | Venus | | |
| IV Emperor | Aries | fire | cardinal |
| V Hierophant | Taurus | earth | fixed |
| VI Lovers | Gemini | air | mutable |
| VII Chariot | Cancer | water | cardinal |
| VIII Strength | Leo | fire | fixed |
| IX Hermit | Virgo | earth | mutable |
| X Wheel | Jupiter | | |
| XI Justice | Libra | air | cardinal |
| XII Hanged Man | *Neptune* | **water** | |
| XIII Death | Scorpio | water | fixed |
| XIV Temperance | Sagittarius | fire | mutable |
| XV Devil | Capricorn | earth | cardinal |
| XVI Tower | Mars: *Pluto* | | |
| XVII Star | Aquarius | air | fixed |
| XVIII Moon | Pisces | water | mutable |
| XIX Sun | Sun | | |
| XX Judgment | *Saturn, Pluto* | **fire** | |
| XXI World | Saturn, spirit: *Earth* | **earth** | |

*Italicized attributions are alternates suggested by author

**Bolded elements are elemental trumps

# ATTRIBUTIONS FOR
# THE MINOR ARCANA: COURT CARDS

| Court Card | Cusp | Modes/Elements |
|---|---|---|
| Queen of Wands | 21° Pisces–20° Aries | mutable water/cardinal fire |
| Knight of Pentacles | 21° Aries–20° Taurus | cardinal fire/fixed earth |
| King of Swords | 21° Taurus–20° Gemini | fixed earth/mutable air |
| Queen of Cups | 21° Gemini–20° Cancer | mutable air/cardinal water |
| Knight of Wands | 21° Cancer–20° Leo | cardinal water/fixed fire |
| King of Pentacles | 21° Leo–20° Virgo | fixed fire/mutable earth |
| Queen of Swords | 21° Virgo–20° Libra | mutable earth/cardinal air |
| Knight of Cups | 21° Libra–20° Scorpio | cardinal air/fixed water |
| King of Wands | 21° Scorpio–20° Sagittarius | fixed water/mutable fire |
| Queen of Pentacles | 21° Sagittarius–20° Capricorn | mutable fire/cardinal earth |
| Knight of Swords | 21° Capricorn–20° Aquarius | cardinal earth/fixed air |
| King of Cups | 21° Aquarius–20° Pisces | fixed air/mutable water |
| Princess of Wands | | fire of earth |
| Princess of Cups | | water of earth |
| Princess of Swords | | air of earth |
| Princess of Pentacles | | earth of earth |

*Note: The attributions of the Kings and Knights of the same suit may be exchanged, i.e. Kings as fixed, Knights as mutable.*

# ATTRIBUTIONS FOR
# THE MINOR ARCANA: PIP CARDS

| Pip Card | Attribution | Mode/Element |
|---|---|---|
| Ace of Wands | primal fire | fire |
| Two of Wands | Mars/Aries | cardinal fire |
| Three of Wands | Sun/Aries | cardinal fire |
| Four of Wands | Venus/Aries | cardinal fire |
| Five of Pentacles | Mercury/Taurus | fixed earth |
| Six of Pentacles | Moon/Taurus | fixed earth |
| Seven of Pentacles | Saturn/Taurus | fixed earth |
| Eight of Swords | Jupiter/Gemini | mutable air |
| Nine of Swords | Mars/Gemini | mutable air |
| Ten of Swords | Sun/Gemini | mutable air |
| Ace of Cups | primal water | water |
| Two of Cups | Venus/Cancer | cardinal water |
| Three of Cups | Mercury/Cancer | cardinal water |
| Four of Cups | Moon/Cancer | cardinal water |
| Five of Wands | Saturn/Leo | fixed fire |
| Six of Wands | Jupiter/Leo | fixed fire |
| Seven of Wands | Mars/Leo | fixed fire |
| Eight of Pentacles | Sun/Virgo | mutable earth |
| Nine of Pentacles | Venus/Virgo | mutable earth |
| Ten of Pentacles | Mercury/Virgo | mutable earth |

| Pip Card | Attribution | Mode/Element |
| --- | --- | --- |
| Ace of Swords | primal air | air |
| Two of Swords | Moon/Libra | cardinal air |
| Three of Swords | Saturn/Libra | cardinal air |
| Four of Swords | Jupiter/Libra | cardinal air |
| Five of Cups | Mars/Scorpio | fixed water |
| Six of Cups | Sun/Scorpio | fixed water |
| Seven of Cups | Venus/Scorpio | fixed water |
| Eight of Wands | Mercury/Sagittarius | mutable fire |
| Nine of Wands | Moon/Sagittarius | mutable fire |
| Ten of Wands | Saturn/Sagittarius | mutable fire |
| Ace of Pentacles | primal earth | earth |
| Two of Pentacles | Jupiter/Capricorn | cardinal earth |
| Three of Pentacles | Mars/Capricorn | cardinal earth |
| Four of Pentacles | Sun/Capricorn | cardinal earth |
| Five of Swords | Venus/Aquarius | fixed air |
| Six of Swords | Mercury/Aquarius | fixed air |
| Seven of Swords | Moon/Aquarius | fixed air |
| Eight of Cups | Saturn/Pisces | mutable water |
| Nine of Cups | Jupiter/Pisces | mutable water |
| Ten of Cups | Mars/Pisces | mutable water |

# PIP CARDS BY ELEMENT

|  | WANDS | CUPS | SWORDS | PENTACLES |
|---|---|---|---|---|
| Aces | Fire | Water | Air | Earth |
| **Cardinal Signs:** | | | | |
| Twos | Mars/Aries | Venus/Cancer | Moon/Libra | Jupiter/Capricorn |
| Threes | Sun/Aries | Mercury/Cancer | Saturn/Libra | Mars/Capricorn |
| Fours | Venus/Aries | Moon/Cancer | Jupiter/Libra | Sun/Capricorn |
| **Fixed Signs:** | | | | |
| Fives | Saturn/Leo | Mars/Scorpio | Venus/Aquarius | Mercury/Taurus |
| Sixes | Jupiter/Leo | Sun/Scorpio | Mercury/Aquarius | Moon/Taurus |
| Sevens | Mars/Leo | Venus/Scorpio | Moon/Aquarius | Saturn/Taurus |
| **Mutable Signs:** | | | | |
| Eights | Mercury/Sagittarius | Saturn/Pisces | Jupiter/Gemini | Sun/Virgo |
| Nines | Moon/Sagittarius | Jupiter/Pisces | Mars/Gemini | Venus/Virgo |
| Tens | Saturn/Sagittarius | Mars/Pisces | Sun/Gemini | Mercury/Virgo |

# PLANETARY DIGNITIES

*Ruler*—"home" sign of planet, natural expression of its energies.

*Detriment*—opposite of sign(s) of rulership; planet struggles to express energies.

*Exaltation*—"happy home" sign of planet, strong/best expression.

*Fall*—opposite sign of exaltation, planet struggles to express energies.

• • •

**Sun:** ☉ rules Leo/in detriment in Aquarius; exalts in Aries/in fall in Libra.

**Moon:** ☽ rules Cancer/in detriment in Capricorn; exalts in Taurus/in fall in Scorpio. Twenty-eight days around Earth; nineteen-year eclipse cycles through zodiac.

**Mercury:** ☿ rules both Gemini and Virgo/in detriment in Sagittarius and Pisces; exalts in Aquarius (or Virgo)/in fall in Leo. Orbits Sun in eighty-eight days.

**Venus:** ♀ rules both Taurus and Libra/in detriment in Scorpio and Aries; exalts in Pisces/in fall in Virgo. Orbits Sun in 225 days.

**Mars:** ♂ rules both Aries and Scorpio/in detriment in Libra and Taurus; exalts in Capricorn/in fall in Cancer. Orbits Sun in 1.8 years.

**Jupiter:** ♃ rules both Sagittarius and Pisces/in detriment in Gemini and Virgo; exalts in Cancer/in fall in Capricorn. Orbits Sun in 11.9 years.

**Saturn:** ♄ rules both Capricorn and Aquarius/in detriment in Cancer and Leo; exalts in Libra/in fall in Aries. Orbits Sun in 29.5 years.

**Uranus:** ♅ co-rules Aquarius/in detriment in Leo; exalts in Scorpio/in fall in Taurus.* Orbits Sun in 84 years.

**Neptune:** ♆ co-rules Pisces/in detriment in Virgo; exalts in Leo/in fall in Aquarius.* Orbits Sun in 165 years.

**Pluto:** ♇ co-rules Scorpio/ in detriment in Taurus; exalts in Aquarius/in fall in Leo.* Orbits Sun in 249 years.

*Please note that with the three outer planets, exaltation and fall are subject to alternate placements.*

# ZODIACAL DIGNITIES

| Zodiac Sign | Glyph | Planetary Ruler | Mode/Element |
|---|---|---|---|
| Aries | ♈ | ♂ | cardinal fire |
| Taurus | ♉ | ♀ | fixed earth |
| Gemini | ♊ | ☿ | mutable air |
| Cancer | ♋ | ☽ | cardinal water |
| Leo | ♌ | ☉ | fixed fire |
| Virgo | ♍ | ☿ | mutable earth |
| Libra | ♎ | ♀ | cardinal air |
| Scorpio | ♏ | ♂ and ♇ | fixed water |
| Sagittarius | ♐ | ♃ | mutable fire |
| Capricorn | ♑ | ♄ | cardinal earth |
| Aquarius | ♒ | ♄ and ♅ | fixed air |
| Pisces | ♓ | ♃ and ♆ | mutable water |

# DIGNITIES OF THE TWELVE HOUSES AND FOUR ELEMENTS

## THE TWELVE HOUSES

| Modality | Houses | Signs |
|---|---|---|
| Cardinal (Angular) | 1, 4, 7, 10 | ♈, ♋, ♎, ♑ |
| Fixed (Succeedent) | 2, 5, 8, 11 | ♉, ♌, ♏, ♒ |
| Mutable (Cadent) | 3, 6, 9, 12 | ♊, ♍, ♐, ♓ |

## THE FOUR ELEMENTS

**Fire**   Ascendant, east, spring equinox
*Houses*: first, fifth, ninth
*Signs*: Aries, Leo, Sagittarius

**Water**   Nadir or IC (*Imum Coeli*), north, summer solstice
*Houses*: fourth, eighth, twelfth
*Signs*: Cancer, Scorpio, Pisces

**Air**   Descendant, west, fall equinox
*Houses*: third, seventh, eleventh
*Signs*: Libra, Aquarius, Gemini

**Earth**   Midheaven or MC (*Midi Coeli*), south, winter solstice
*Houses*: second, sixth, tenth
*Signs*: Capricorn, Taurus, Virgo

# LOCATIONAL DIGNITIES
## HOROSCOPE-FORM DIAGRAM

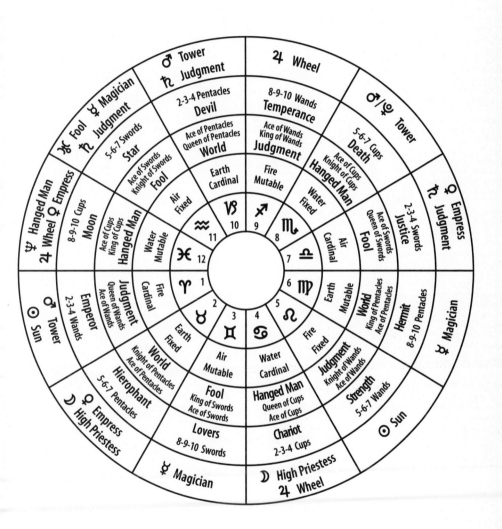

# BIBLIOGRAPHY

Agrippa, Henry Cornelius. *Three Books of Occult Philosophy*. Translated by James Freake, edited by Donald Tyson. St. Paul, Minn.: Llewellyn, 2000.

Crowley, Aleister. *The Book of Thoth (Egyptian Tarot)*. New York: U.S. Games Systems, Inc., 1969.

Etteilla. *Manière de se récréer avec le jeu de cartes nommées tarots (How to Have Fun with the Deck of Cards Called Tarot)*. Amsterdam and Paris: Segault & Legras, 1785.

Garrison, Omar V. *Tantra: The Yoga of Sex*. New York: Julian Press/Crown Publishing Group, 1964.

Graves, Robert. *The Greek Myths: Complete Edition*. New York: Penguin Books, 1955.

Greene, Liz, and Howard Sasportas. *The Inner Planets: Building Blocks of Personal Reality*. York Beach, Maine: Weiser, 1993.

Harris, Lady Frieda, and Aleister Crowley. *The Thoth Tarot*. Stamford, CT: U.S. Games Systems, Inc. and A. G. Muller and CIE, 1969.

Hazel, Elizabeth, and James Revak. "The First Systematic Integration of Tarot and Astrology: Etteilla's Correspondences and Divinatory Method." *The Tarot Journal* 2, no. 1 (spring 2002): 15-31. www.villarevak.org/astro/main.html.

Jackson, Nigel. *The Nigel Jackson Tarot*. St. Paul, Minn.: Llewellyn, 2000.

Javane, Faith, and Dusty Bunker. *Numerology and the Divine Triangle*. Atglen, Pa.: Whitford Press, 1979.

Jones, Marthy. *It's in the Cards.* York Beach, Maine: Weiser, 1984.

Jung, Carl. *The Archetypes and the Collective Unconscious.* Bollingen Series XX, Volume 9, Part I. Princeton: Princeton Univ. Press, 1969.

Jung, Carl. *The Portable Jung.* Edited by Joseph Campbell. New York: Penguin Books/Viking Press, 1971.

Lewis, James. *The Astrology Encyclopedia.* Detroit: Visible Ink/Gale Research Inc., 1994.

Lilly, William. *Christian Astrology.* 1647 Reprint, London: Regulus Publishing/Ascella, 1985.

Morris, Desmond. *The Human Zoo.* New York: McGraw-Hill, 1969.

Opsopaus, John. *The Pythagorean Tarot.* St. Paul, Minn.: Llewellyn, 2001.

Smith, Pamela Colman. *Rider-Waite-Smith Tarot.* Stamford, Conn.: U.S. Games Systems, Inc., 1993.

# INDEX

# ABOUT THE AUTHOR

PHOTO CREDIT: DEREK SANDERSON

Elizabeth Hazel has been immersed in astrology and tarot for over thirty years. She specializes in combining these forecasting tools in innovate ways and has done extensive writing on this topic, as well as on other forms of divination, history, and mythology. Her articles have appeared in the *Tarot Journal*, *ITS News*, the *ATA Quarterly*, *Tarot Passages*, *SageWoman* magazine, *Circle News*, and the NCGR Memberletter.

For two decades, Liz has been educating consumers on how to select reputable practitioners and get the most out of their readings. She has also been a participant at many tarot conferences around the country and hopes that the tarot community will eventually become as vital and supportive as the astrology community.

Her other interests include perfumery and gardening and she is an award-winning composer, performer, and artist. Liz lives in a Historic Register neighborhood in Toledo, Ohio and is currently working on another book dedicated to exploring tarot-astrology techniques.

# TO OUR READERS

Weiser Books, an imprint of Red Wheel/Weiser, publishes books across the entire spectrum of occult and esoteric subjects. Our mission is to publish quality books that will make a difference in people's lives without advocating any one particular path or field of study. We value the integrity, originality, and depth of knowledge of our authors.

Our readers are our most important resource, and we value your input, suggestions, and ideas about what you would like to see published. Please feel free to contact us, to request our latest book catalog, or to be added to our mailing list.

RED WHEEL/WEISER, LLC
P.O. Box 612
York Beach, ME 03910-0612
*www.redwheelweiser.com*